A LEG TO STAND ON

To Annette —

Life is a moment best shared with a dog.

A LEG TO STAND ON

A Shared Journey of Healing

TIMOTHY MCHENRY

iUniverse, Inc.
Bloomington

A Leg to Stand On
A Shared Journey of Healing

Copyright © 2012 by Timothy McHenry.

All rights reserved. No part of this book may be used or reproduced by any means, graphic, electronic, or mechanical, including photocopying, recording, taping or by any information storage retrieval system without the written permission of the publisher except in the case of brief quotations embodied in critical articles and reviews.

iUniverse books may be ordered through booksellers or by contacting:

iUniverse
1663 Liberty Drive
Bloomington, IN 47403
www.iuniverse.com
1-800-Authors (1-800-288-4677)

Because of the dynamic nature of the Internet, any web addresses or links contained in this book may have changed since publication and may no longer be valid. The views expressed in this work are solely those of the author and do not necessarily reflect the views of the publisher, and the publisher hereby disclaims any responsibility for them.

Any people depicted in stock imagery provided by Thinkstock are models, and such images are being used for illustrative purposes only.
Certain stock imagery © Thinkstock.

ISBN: 978-1-4759-5143-1 (sc)
ISBN: 978-1-4759-5264-3 (hc)
ISBN: 978-1-4759-5144-8 (ebk)

Library of Congress Control Number: 2012918312

Printed in the United States of America

iUniverse rev. date: 10/29/2012

CONTENTS

Acknowledgements ix
Foreword by Dixie: A Moment in Time xiii
Introduction xv

Chapter 1: The Other Side 1
Insights: Dixie the "Tie-Down" Dog 5
Chapter 2: Highway 24 8
Chapter 3: Dixie's Angels 12
Chapter 4: Smitten 16
Chapter 5: Betty Jo 18
Insights: Am I Going Home Today? 21
Chapter 6: The Lucky Ones 22
Chapter 7: Finding the Inner Dog 25
Chapter 8: Poster Girl 28
Chapter 9: Lightning Strikes 33
Chapter 10: Teamwork 36
Chapter 11: An Empty Space 41
Chapter 12: The Accusation 46
Insights: Where Are You? 53
Chapter 13: Missing In Action 55
Insights: "I Am For You" 65
Chapter 14: Tim the Trainer 68

Chapter 15: From Bad to Worse 73

Chapter 16: Lost in the Desert 76

Insights: Lonely But Not Alone 81

Chapter 17: Soul For Sale 84

Chapter 18: Afraid 104

Chapter 19: Ground Zero 109

Chapter 20: We, the Jury 114

Chapter 21: Vindication 121

Chapter 22: Prodigal Sons 125

Chapter 23: A Chink in the Armor 128

Chapter 24: Clean Running 134

Insights: My Favorite Things 142

Chapter 25: For Josh 146

Chapter 26: Who Says You Can't Come Home? 156

Chapter 27: Lights, Camera . . . Really? 160

Chapter 28: The Gift 163

Insights: Look What Followed You Home! 169

Chapter 29: Dropping In and Out 171

Chapter 30: Not Again 174

Chapter 31: Symbiosis 181

Chapter 32: Pet Trainer Chronicles 189

Insights: I Am Not Your Fur Baby! 192

Chapter 33: Hero Worship 195

Chapter 34: The Soul of a Dog 200

Chapter 35: Forever in a Moment 205

Dixie's Appendix 211

To Mom: You always said I should and you believed that I could.

To all the Dixie Dogs who shine their light into the darkness and show us the way.

ACKNOWLEDGEMENTS

Of the gifts we receive in this world, friends are the most cherished. Brian, Phil, and Dustin have listened patiently to my rants about this project while secretly wondering if I was going to pull it off. Your copy is in the mail. Postage due, of course.

Ten percent of the profits earned from the sale of this book will be donated to Helping Hands Humane Society of Topeka, Kansas. You chose life for a "disposable dog" named Dixie. In a sense, you saved two lives that day. These miracles happen in shelters and within rescue organizations each day. If the message in this book inspires you to share your life with a pet, adopt, don't shop.

After a particularly difficult time in my life, a dear friend gave me a framed photograph of a half-opened barn door leading to a sun drenched field of green. It was a metaphor for my life at that time. PetSmart was that door in terms of my career. "Tim the Trainer" didn't exist until you came along.

Thanks to the hundreds of people who have taken my pet training classes over the past six years. I'm a better trainer for having known you and your wonderful dogs. I would be negligent (not to mention in deep doo-doo) if I didn't acknowledge the many PetSmart associates and managers who have been my extended family these past several years. Something borrowed, something gained.

Timothy McHenry

Merriam-Webster defines memoir as "a narrative composed of personal experience." Suffice to say this genre requires little research by the author. What I have done is consumed every doggie memoir and novel I could find for the past two years. There are some great ones out there that have moved me and cured acute cases of writer's block. Here are the best of the best:

"A Dog's Purpose" and "A Dog's Journey," W. Bruce Cameron
"Pack of Two," Caroline Knapp
"Until Tuesday," Luis Carlos Montalvan
"Merle's Door," Ted Kerasote
"Marley and Me," John Grogan
"The Art of Racing in the Rain," Garth Stein
"A Big Little Life," Dean Koontz
"Love is the Best Medicine," Dr. Nick Trout
"The Other End of the Leash," and "For the Love of a Dog," Patricia McConnell
"Always Allie," Dr. Kipp Van Camp

After pricing various editing services, I "hired" (perhaps "coerced" is a more accurate term) good friend and grammar police chief Veronica Caine to dissect the manuscript. In exchange, I help her with Sir Barks-a-Lot (a/k/a Romeo the Schnauzer) and gift wrapped a bottle of Skinny Girl Cucumber Vodka. A barter economy certainly works for me.

For the record, some names were changed to protect the young, the inept and those whose reputations might be damaged by the truth. You know who you are.

The Bradford Pet Hospital team led by Dr. Jed Barnes has been in our corner since 2006. Best care anywhere.

Dixie's continued success in the agility ring can be attributed to the gentle tutelage of Lotta Sydanmaa and weekly practice sessions at Dog Obedience Group (D.O.G.) in Blue Springs, Mo. We've made some wonderful new friends. Thanks for including us in the agility exhibitions where Dixie can play to the crowd.

In 2012, long time journalism advisor Duane Shufelberger was voted into the Topeka West High Hall of Fame. Mr. Shuf, you entered my Hall of Fame 34 years ago.

My dogs Dixie and Oreo have been my constant companions during this journey not to mention my inspiration. Patiently you maintained a vigil as I muddled through another chapter and umpteen revisions hoping I wouldn't forget that morning walk or excursion to the dog park. I could not and I would not have done this without you. Somehow I think you know that.

And finally to my beloved son Josh; may you find the path that one day leads you home.

FOREWORD BY DIXIE: A MOMENT IN TIME

For a moment I was a puppy so young that I could not see or hear. My focus was on one thing; the sweet nectar that came from my mother. I could smell it and I inched my way along the softness until I felt its warmth ease down my throat. There is no before. No after. Only now.

For a moment I open my eyes and feel Tim's fingers lightly massage the wisps of hair just under my ear. I am happy and the corners of his mouth turn upward. I have learned it is a good thing when people look at you in this way. This is how we start each day. He is thinking only of me and I am thinking only of him. We exist in this perfect moment together.

There was a time when Tim's corners rarely turned that way. In those days they pointed downward. His cheeks were hollow and his shoulders hunched forward. Sadness oozed from his pores. You could smell it a block away. A dog's job is to try and bring to bring comfort and joy to those moments. I spin in circles and he walks me. I pant and nudge the leash with my nose and we go to the dog park. Sometimes my leg hurts if we walk or jog too much but I never let on because he relaxes more when we're moving. I hate chasing the ball only to bring it back so I can fetch it again. It makes Tim smile so I do it anyway. Other times I curl up with him even though it means hopping into a chair that is much too small for us both. The sadness gives way and the moment is all about love. Yes, I can smell that too. It's the greatest of all the feelings.

Timothy McHenry

In this moment we are hiking and I stop to take in the fragrance left behind by a deer. The air is much cooler now and Tim also pauses and admires the strange colors of the leaves. His senses, dull in comparison to mine, are focused on the tree and he forgets about things he cannot control. This is what it's like to be a dog. Sometimes I stop even when there is nothing interesting to smell because I know Tim will take a break and experience the moment the way that I do. He's going to make a great dog someday but we still have some work to do.

The glowing screen in the living room places Tim in a moment he will never really experience first-hand. This is not healthy so I groan and push his hand upwards so he will return to this moment and pet me. Humans spend so much time wishing for things they see on the screen when they have all they need right in front of them.

Moments of sadness are not limited to people. Sometimes it is the human that brings comfort and joy to the dog. This book is about a journey of mutual healing that Tim and I shared. It is not a story unique to people and dogs. We have been caring for one another before there were books to read.

I am a very old dog. Older than you know. There will be a moment when I leave this body. It's happened before. I will not know where I am going until the moment I arrive but I am certain that Tim will be there . . .

In just a moment.

INTRODUCTION

Nowadays my moniker reads "Tim the Trainer." A PetSmart manager tagged me with that because there was another guy named Tim working in the store. My students picked it up and it has been my e-mail address since 2006. I prefer to think of myself as a "pet educator." It's not the dogs that usually need the training.

The first 25 years of my professional career, however, was spent in youth development. I spent 16 years with Big Brothers/Big Sisters in various locales. I've done crisis mediation with children and families. When my son Josh was born in 1994, my passion turned to early education. I was Mr. Tim, the "kid guy." The career change was not planned but it was inspired by an extraordinary dog named Dixie.

As a teen I noticed that kids naturally gravitated towards me. Occasionally, extended family would roll into town or friends of my parents would stop by and I was the self-appointed playmate for the children. Adults were complimentary of my ability to entertain—a side of my personality suppressed by a disapproving father.

Baseball was my focus as an adolescent but a head injury put me on the shelf for a good part of one season. Dad was a great coach but forgot the part about teaching me to duck at a high and tight fastball. While rehabilitating from a concussion and an inner ear imbalance, Dad suggested I help his friend coach a little league baseball team. The team finished the year undefeated and a coach was born.

I was never the same player after the head injury and a once promising baseball career came to an abrupt halt when I was 17. I continued to coach. Someone once remarked that I had a "way" with kids and for some reason I connected better with them than with my peers. Years of work in youth development and a marriage eventually followed.

I became a single parent when my son was two. Juggling a career and being a full time parent is not for the faint of heart. When I made time to read, I wanted to be inspired. I wanted to feel the full spectrum of emotion. I wanted to laugh. And yes, I expected to cry. Maybe that's why my favorite books have always been about dogs. Read a story featuring a dog and you're sure to be hopping on an emotional roller coaster full of hairpin turns, steep climbs, and plunges that will take your breath away. Live with a dog, love a dog, and you pretty much get the same thing. What binds us to these creatures is a love free of conditions and expectations. It is void of pettiness and premeditation.

We all know there is one inescapable truth about a dog book. The dog dies. Books about dogs are like Halloween haunted houses. You learn to proceed at your own risk. As the story builds to a climax, we know to holster our emotions in preparation for the inevitable. Still, we keep reading, tip toeing through an emotional mine field. Anyone who's ever been in a car wreck knows the feeling. You catch a glimpse of the people hauler as it cruises through a yellow caution light. Your light is green and you ease into the intersection. Suddenly real time slows to a crawl as the truck draws a bead on the side of your sedan. In your book, the dog gets old and frail.

Impact! You feel as though someone dropped a barbell on your chest. It's the same sensation you experience when the dog you have grown more attached to with each turn of the page invariably dies. You saw it coming but could do nothing to prevent it. That lump in your throat soon becomes an airway obstruction and you swallow forcefully to catch the next breath. You swear you'll never read another story about a dog.

Let's face it. The only downside to loving dogs is that they don't live long enough. Still, most of us continue to bring them into our homes and into our hearts throughout our lives. What does that say about us? Perhaps more importantly, what does it say about them? For the record, the dog named Dixie does not die. There now, don't you feel better already?

As a matter of fact, Dixie insisted on adding her own unique "insights" into the final manuscript. How could I tell her no when her face garnishes the front cover?

Obviously I was not privy to the conversations that took place before Dixie came into my life. Hopefully, I've captured the essence of them in the early chapters of this book, for they tell a story of compassion and generosity that abound in the world of animal rescue. Sadly, such gestures are in decline elsewhere.

Nothing stokes the fire in my soul quite like the perfect blend of poetry and melody regardless of genre. Music is truly a universal language. Perhaps some of the lyrics that christen these chapters have been taken out of context. If so, I apologize to the gifted artists who may have had some greater purpose for their music. Please take comfort in knowing that your insightful words bring a greater understanding to our message of love and redemption.

"I will be the answer
At the end of the line
I will be there for you
While you take the time . . ."

Sarah McLachlan, "Answer"

CHAPTER 1: THE OTHER SIDE

It was my fault for letting Princess wander off leash but she hardly posed a threat. The senseless act of brutality that ensued served as a reminder that our species is not nearly as evolved as we believe. Her ear-piercing scream could be heard from a block away. There were no emergency vet clinics available. I made her as comfortable as I could and slept with her on the floor that night. X-rays the next morning revealed a compound fracture and she was immediately taken into surgery where a steel rod was implanted to reconnect the severed bone. My vet said that Princess had likely been kicked, possibly by someone wielding a heavy leather boot.

As the years passed, Princess began to favor the leg after long hikes or jogs. It was especially painful in the winter. We lived in Topeka, Kansas and midwestern winters can be harsh. One day in the spring of 2001, we took a walk around a small lake when she suddenly collapsed and would not budge. I was initially irked, thinking she was tired and just being stubborn so nudged her from behind to get her moving. It was clear that she was in some distress. I wound up carrying her 60 pounds for nearly a mile then drove her to Dr. Larry Fischer at Western Hills Veterinary Clinic straightaway.

Dr. Fischer was an experienced veterinarian with strong Christian beliefs. He had seen thousands of dogs in his career but always managed to make me feel like Princess was his only patient. I liked that about him. X-rays were taken, blood was drawn. A day later Dr. Fischer called and asked that I come to the clinic to discuss the results. His reluctance to share details over the phone had me concerned and I spent a restless night fearing the worst.

The worst was what I got. Cancer had been hibernating in Princess like a famished grizzly bear for years. It was bone cancer, likely perpetuated by the leg injury. She had less than six months. Medication could keep the pain at bay but nothing could cure or slow the spread. Over the next three months, I stood by helplessly as this once vibrant dog labored to her bowl for dinner. By August, Princess was dragging her hindquarters across the yard and could not maintain a stand long enough to have a bowel movement. I sat with her in the shade and looked deep into disconsolate eyes. We both knew it was time.

I called Dr. Fischer's office and the appointment was scheduled for the following day. You go to the dentist and tell the receptionist that you're there to have a cavity filled. What was I going to say to Dr. Fischer's receptionist tomorrow? This is Princess and she is here to die? How surreal it was to schedule the end of a life. I wonder how that looks in the appointment book. How does the staff at the clinic approach each day knowing that a beloved pet is going to sleep a 3 p.m. and never waking up? These rhetorical thoughts swam through my head in the hours that preceded our appointment with destiny.

My son Josh was only seven then. I had been a single custodial parent for five years. Josh and I were a pack of two. We lost my father just four years back and now Josh was dealing with death again. I spoke to him in hushed tones as we ate breakfast. He knew of the cancer and had sounded the alarm every time Princess collapsed under her own weight. I tried to avoid the euphemisms that only served to make me feel better. "We have to do what's right. "She'll be going to a better place." "God has a plan for her." "The dogs in heaven need a new friend."

Rather, I explained exactly what was to happen later that day.

"Princess and I are going to see Dr. Fischer. He will give her some medicine to make her sleepy, then inject her with a drug that will stop her heart. Princess will feel no pain from the needle and cancer can never hurt her again. After you say goodbye, you will not see Princess again in this life. But her memory will be in your heart forever—just like with Grandpa."

Then there were tears. Josh was a sweet, sensitive boy who spontaneously wept for months over the loss of his Grandpa though he was only three at the time. I held him as we shared memories of our sweet girl under the shade of a silver maple tree. Her face was sunken and the skin around her hips had grown taut. She had barely eaten in days. I told my son of our hikes in the Arizona mountains before he was but a twinkle in my eye. There was the time at the lake where Princess caught a frog and nearly gagged when the little green guy secreted some hideous tasting goo from his pores in an attempt to flee his clueless captor. There were the horror film reactions to her classic "grin." I reminded Josh that Princess had been like a shepherd when he was a baby, sleeping under his crib and coming out to the living room only to reprimand me for not being more attentive when he cried or awakened from a nap.

I had arranged for a friend to watch Josh for the afternoon. Though the appointment was only booked for 20 minutes, I was not sure what time I would feel like coming home.

It was time to go.

Josh cried as only children can and hugged Princess for the last time. I loaded her carefully in a kennel that was secured in the bed of my compact pickup. Our appointment was at 2 p.m. but I left at one. Princess and I were going to visit her favorite places one last time. There was the Shunga Trail that bordered the creek by the same name. We stopped and admired the majestic maples and oaks at Gage Park. From there, we cruised up to the Governor's mansion where public trails encircled a pond. She loved to swim out to the center and wreak havoc with the resident ducks. It was on that trail the Princess laid down, forcing me to carry her back to the car. It was to be the last hike we would take together.

We pulled into the cemetery where Dad is buried. That was always such a peaceful walk. I found it morbidly ironic that a cemetery would be our last stop before our appointment with death. Each time the truck came to a halt at a familiar place, Princess struggled to her feet as if to inhale one last moment.

I arrived at Western Hills Veterinary Clinic. She knew and was afraid. I opened the tailgate kennel to find that she had soiled her kennel. Princess never did that. I gently lifted her from the back of the truck and carried her into the waiting room. We were a mess. The nurse took one look and immediately escorted us back to the bathing area. I hoisted Princess into the tub and the nurse gently rinsed her off and shampooed her coat while I cleaned up. She was thoroughly dried and brushed. Thanks to Dr. Fischer's compassionate staff, Princess was going to leave this world with her dignity intact.

Dr. Fischer entered the exam room and asked how I was doing. Curious question, as I wasn't the one facing the needle. I nearly lost it at that point and could only nod my head. I had to be strong for Princess and for Josh so kept the tear ducts on hold. Dr. Fischer placed his hand on my shoulder to steady me while he administered the first injection. Princess was already lying down and I could feel her body start to relax as the sedative took hold.

I remember Dr. Fischer asking if I had any questions. I shook my head, as he had already explained the procedure. I stroked Princess' beautiful yellow coat and whispered "I love you, sweet girl."

"I'll see you on the other side," Dr. Fischer said as he administered the final injection.

I stroked the side of my girl's face and laid my head on her rib cage as she peacefully took her last breath. One minute she was alive. The next she was gone. And in that precise moment throughout the world, there were births, wedding proposals, arguments, couples in the throes of passion, cell calls, text messages, the honking of horns at busy intersections, clocks being punched, dreams dreamt. And death.

But in this moment none of that mattered. My Princess was gone and I released a tsunami of anguish bottled up since my dad died. I had been told the exam room was mine for the afternoon and it was well over an hour before I could bring myself to abandon Princess' lifeless body on the exam table and drive home. It would be four years before I was ready to be in relationship with a dog again. And that dog was Dixie, a yellow lab. Just like Princess. Only not.

INSIGHTS: DIXIE THE "TIE-DOWN" DOG

Sometimes I wish I wasn't a dog. People don't chase rabbits. They don't get tingly all over when those demonic creatures raise their fuzzy white tails and take flight. I was once a "tie-down" dog. A tie-down dog spends his life wearing a chain around his neck. The other end is connected to a big stick that humans twist into the ground. My chain was cruel. It allowed me chase the rodents that danced across our lawn until I got close enough to smell their breath. Without warning, it snapped me back, sometimes flipping me over in the process as the critter scampered away. Rabbits, squirrels, and other varmints were placed on this earth to torment dogs. Of this I am certain. Their cackling is all I had for company. I was so lonely.

Like most tie-down dogs, I was once allowed inside. Sometimes I peed in the house when no one was near to take me outside. I tried to hold it. Really I did. But they never came around so I became a tie-down dog. The man brought me food and water once a day. His mate yelled at me through the window when I barked a hello at the neighbor kids.

She had to be the dumbest bunny that ever hopped. There she was, sitting there just a few feet away. My ears perked, my mouth closed. This moron was begging to be caught. I lunged. She froze for a moment and then turned towards the bushes but I was too fast and cut her off. Suddenly she darted towards the street and I forgot about the chain. I felt it tighten around my neck but his time I was not jerked backwards. There was a loud snap as my collar fell to the ground. Suddenly there was blast of noise and a screeching sound. A searing jolt of pain ran up my left front leg and I screamed.

Everything was a blur after that. I vaguely remember the man wrapping a cloth around my leg and looping the chain around my neck. Rabbits, birds, and squirrels went about their business but I was in no mood to chase. My leg was on fire and there was no water to put it out so I laid on the yellow grass and tried not to think about it.

Two days had passed and I could not take my mind off the pain. The woman wrapped more cloth around my leg but it turned red just as quickly as the first one did. Usually I try to eat before the flies land on my breakfast but today I didn't care. I was thirsty but did not drink. Moving to the water bowl meant standing and that caused my leg to throb even more. I secretly wished I didn't have that stupid leg anymore. Dogs are really three legged animals with a spare. Maybe it would just come off if I chewed carefully around the cloth.

The flies had left my food and were now buzzing around my leg. Flies like blood and I was a lunch buffet. It hurt to chew on my leg but I kept at it. Finally the man came out to check on me. He seemed shocked at what he saw and unfastened my chain. Could I be going back inside? As it turned out, we took a car ride. Cars and I were not on speaking terms so I was not happy about this. After several minutes, I was carried into a large building with what sounded like a million barking dogs. The man walked away but I was too tired and sore to follow him.

A woman that smelled like soap carried me to a kennel and gently lowered me onto a warm blanket. Best of all, there was no chain. She gave me water and I lapped it up. Some food was left in a bowl but there was too much pain to feel hunger. I curled up against the wall and tried to relax. A man approached me cautiously while an older woman stood behind him with a look of concern on her face. I could sense the fear he was trying to suppress though I did not understand it. I was a good dog and had never hurt a human. He ran his fingers down my damaged leg. It hurt when he moved my leg so I tried to blink the pain away. He stroked my fur with his soft hands then smiled as he backed away. The man returned and placed a needle into my skin. It stung a bit but it was nothing compared to what I was already feeling. My leg began to numb and the hurt faded. My eyes grew heavy.

Although there were dogs and kind people everywhere, I never felt so alone. What was to become of me? Would the pain ever stop? A dark wave of sadness rushed over me as I drifted off to sleep.

> *"The long and winding road that leads to your door*
> *Will never disappear*
> *I've seen that road before it always leads me here*
> *Leads me to your door . . ."*
>
> John Lennon/Paul McCartney, "The Long and Winding Road"

CHAPTER 2: HIGHWAY 24

One of the moments that defined my life took place in late October of 2005. I was the director of Christ the King Early Education Center in Topeka, Kansas. The local Archdiocese had called a meeting in Kansas City to roll out its new benefit package and I was required to attend. For the record, I despise meetings. That wasn't what I signed on for when I chose a career in youth services. I wanted to work with young people. This meeting would have all the charm of a crocodile with an abscessed tooth. At least I could take solace in the splendor of a Kansas fall as the miles slipped away.

It had been some time since I lived with a dog and the longing had returned. Princess was truly a gem. The cancer that took her life in 2001 also removed any desire to live the nightmare of losing a best friend. But for reasons I cannot explain to this day, I felt it was time and I was consumed by a yearning I did not understand. Highway 24 would make for a scenic drive back to the center and assistant director Angie had things well under control as was always the case in my absence. The two-lane would take me right by Helping Hands Humane Society where I had volunteered for several years socializing dogs in the play yard. No messages from Meadows Elementary. Josh was 11 now and safely tucked away at school. I had all the bases covered.

I was looking for Princess both in form and in temperament. No puppies. I had never been particularly good at the potty training thing with

Princess. I had managed to get my son out of pull ups by his first day of kindergarten so figured I had reached the toileting summit. No point in climbing that mountain again.

As usual, the shelter was full—and loud. That much had not changed since I walked these corridors. Driven to a state of frenzy by their incarceration, the poor souls leaped, barked, and twirled mindlessly as I ambled by.

Surely someone will love this dog, I thought.

The harsh reality was a walk down the proverbial Green Mile for more than half of these animals. A quick sedative followed by a needle prick. Another nameless life lost to make room for another whose fate would be decided in a matter of days.

Deep down you bleed for them all but you have to check those emotions at the front door if you ever intend to find not "a" dog but "the" dog. Until this day Princess had been that dog. She was my jogging partner, the nanny for my son, and my counsel during the barren years following my divorce and the death of my father. Could there be another dog such as she? Would finding that dog cause me to abandon my memories of our hikes down the Shunga trail?

Don't think so much. Just walk. If that dog is out there, he or she will find you and shoot an arrow straight into your heart. Be patient. It may not be today but perhaps one day soon.

I stopped dead in my tracks.

There she was.

A petite yellow Lab mix, a much darker shade of yellow than Princess, sat pressed against the back wall of the kennel. I stopped. Our eyes met. Hers were soulful, intelligent, yet sad in a way I would come to understand in my own life. The arrow she pulled from her quiver had found its mark.

Then she moved. Not like a dog but more like a kangaroo. Hopping. She lurched with obvious discomfort but never took those shiny copper eyes off me for a second. I was mesmerized at her approach but managed to glance downward long enough to notice that there was no left front leg. No stump—nothing. It was gone. A fresh scar, pink and pronounced, zipped the skin together across her shoulder. Given the bruising along her rib cage, I concluded that this was no birth defect. The leg had been recently amputated.

I reached through the kennel door to touch her muzzle while she explored my fingers with her snout. She rested her head against the chain link and though my curiosity burned I found myself unable to sever the eye contact between us. Linear time had ceased and I was not ready for this moment to end. Questions. There were so many questions. I sighed, collected myself, and walked briskly past the now invisible faces of the other dogs to see an adoption counselor. I had to know the story.

Shelter manager Stacey was sitting at her steel desk at Helping Hands Humane Society when I walked into the lobby.

"What can you tell me about the dog in North 62," I asked.

"Which is one is that?" she replied as she browsed through a three ring binder

"Geez lady, how many dogs with three legs do you typically have available for adoption on the third Wednesday in October?" I wondered silently.

The corners of Stacey's face turned upward as she scanned the page in front of her.

"Ahh, that's Dixie. She's pretty special. She just needs someone to love her."

I secretly hoped that someone would be me.

"What's her story?" I inquired, not knowing that the same question would be asked of me hundreds of times over the next seven years.

"I'm going to get Carol. She can tell you more."

And with that, Stacey abruptly got up and disappeared through a door that led to the office of the shelter director Carol Stubbs. Carol emerged from her tiny office and she recognized me right away.

"Are you here for Dixie?"

I hesitated—"well—I have some questions."

Before I could utter the first of them, Carol explained that Dixie was surrendered by her owner over a week ago. According to the intake report, she had been hit by a car, then tied up and left in the yard for three days with an injury that clearly required immediate attention. As the story goes, Dixie was thought to have caught a rabbit on the morning of the third day because she was chewing on something bloody. The owners signed her over to Helping Hands when it was clear that the extent of her injury would require more veterinary care than they could afford.

Dixie's arrival presented Carol and Stacey with an agonizing decision faced by shelter directors every day. An amputation might cost $2,500. Helping Hands had $800 left in its medical care budget. Dixie's very survival came down to economics. Allocating the remainder of the medical fund on one dog would break the bank. Unlike governments, animal shelters won't be in business long if they run in the red. It was October. Depleting the medical fund on one dog would leave nothing available for the next Dixie. And the one after that. And the one after that.

Dixie was a deemed a disposable dog.

"You're in the arms of the angel
May you find some comfort here . . ."

Sarah McLachlan, "Angel"

CHAPTER 3: DIXIE'S ANGELS

Dr. Darrell Carder opened Stonehouse Animal Clinic in 2004. A graduate of Kansas State University, Dr. Carder had been practicing veterinary medicine for thirty some years and had a soft spot for shelter animals. As fate would have it, Dr. Carder was on call with Helping Hands Humane Society the day that Dixie was brought in.

Once processed through intake, Dixie was taken to a kennel in a small room where injured strays were placed apart from the rest of the shelter population. Dixie lay huddled against the back of the kennel, her head resting across a grossly swollen left front paw. Blood and torn tissue dangled from what used to be her toes. The lower third of her left front leg looked as though it had been run through a sausage grinder. Though in horrific pain, her face was solemn yet dignified. Carol and Stacey approached slowly. The behaviors of an injured and frightened dog can be most unpredictable. Despite years of experience with injured animals, the women were taking no chances. Carol extended her hand and Dixie sniffed. She knew it was safe to move closer and she reached down to stroke Dixie's fur. The wounded dog remained remarkably composed.

"Let's call Dr. Carder. He needs to take a look at this."

Locally, Carol is recognized as that warm hearted lady who appears on television holding a shelter animal and imploring the public to come and adopt. Carol introduced every critter as though it were her very own with passion and grace. I am convinced that all the animals she brought to the small screen were eventually adopted out. You could change the channel but you simply could not dismiss her.

Dr. Carder, Stacey, and Carol met outside the kennel as Dixie's life hung in the balance.

"This dog is amazing," Carol said. She has been so calm since they brought her in and you know she is in agony. I hate the idea of having to put her down. Just look at those eyes."

Dr. Carder smiled and entered the kennel. He had a sixth sense about these things.

"This dog is a keeper," he thought as he began his examination.

Dixie lay prone on her right side with the damaged leg extended. Stacey comforted Dixie as Dr. Carder began to palpitate the misshaped limb. Dixie was muzzled as a precaution but not once did she nip or demonstrate any outward signs of aggression. Carol folded her arms and waited patiently in the kennel doorway for a word from Dr. Carder.

"I need to get her back to the hospital and get some x-rays. The tissue damage is extensive and I'm pretty sure there is a fracture not to mention some muscle and tendon damage."

Carol pressed her lips together and gave Dr. Carder a nod of acknowledgement. With a depleted medical fund, this was not what she wanted to hear.

"I'll let you know," Dr. Carder said he placed Dixie on a cart and wheeled her out to his car.

It was 4:30 and Carol's work day was nearly over. She had come in at 7 am that October morning to catch up on some administrative "to-dos" while the phones were quiet. Though weary, she could not bring herself to leave until she had heard from Dr. Carder. There would be no sleep in the Stubbs household tonight until Dixie's fate was determined so Carol busied herself with mindless filing for the next hour.

The call from Dr. Carder's office came much too quickly.

"Hi Carol, its Dr. Carder. She's going to lose the leg."

Carol's heart plunged to the pit of her stomach. It was surely a death sentence for Dixie. Next came something totally incongruent with the moment—a chuckle from Dr. Carder.

"Every time I examine one of your animals, you tell me the same thing. 'He's a great dog' or 'she's a great cat.' Well, you were right about this one. This is an extraordinary dog. I'll do the amputation for $200. Can you live with that?"

Suddenly the gloom that threatened to culminate the day was lifted like an anvil from Carol's narrow shoulders.

"I don't know what to say. Yes! YES!"

And so it was done. The procedure took nearly two hours. Dixie's vital signs remained strong throughout and it was a routine as an amputation could be. Dixie was young. Dr. Carder put her age at about a year and a half. It's always an educated guess with a shelter dog.

Stonehouse is open round the clock and Dixie's condition was monitored closely by nurses throughout the night. By the next morning, she was fully alert with a zipper-like incision across her left shoulder blade. A purple blemish formed around the scar that extended down a good portion of Dixie's torso. She refused food for the first couple of days.

Though given generous doses of pain controlling medication, Dixie's movements in her kennel were labored. Each trek outdoors with hospital staff to empty her bladder and bowel was both excruciating and exhausting. When she stumbled, it always meant landing on her scar which sent ripples of pain through her body. She was disoriented, confused, and everything hurt. Worst of all, she was alone.

Dixie was ready to return to Helping Hands Humane Society by week's end. Her recovery had been remarkable though it came as no surprise to Dr. Carder. The smiling vet greeted Carol at the intake door.

"Didn't I tell you this one was special?" Dr. Carder said as he handed the leash over to Carol.

"Yes, she replied noting the tone of irony. "You always say that."

Love is you
You and me
Love is knowing
We can be"

John Lennon, "Love"

CHAPTER 4: SMITTEN

I knew nothing about dogs with three legs. Since then I have come to understand that I knew very little about dogs, period. Sadly, I shared this ignorance with many well intended but clueless keepers of canines. Sure, I had grown up with dogs, but as with most kids, I had taken little responsibility for their care. Our dachshunds Hans and Hilde were fixtures in our household. Mom and Dad fed them, cleaned up after them, gave them baths, walked them and took them to the vet. My job was to love on them and I did that with great earnest.

"Would you like to meet Dixie in one of or visitation rooms?" Stacey asked.

"Yes—please!" I replied, trying to curb my enthusiasm (and failing miserably).

I took a seat in a room about the size of an airline lavatory not quite knowing what to expect. In many ways it reminded me the hours before my son Josh was born. There was a sense that the moments ahead would be life changing.

I have long acknowledged that I am the nurturing type. The thought of rehabilitating this incredible dog with three legs intrigued me to no end. Yet I was cautious and did not verbally commit to Dixie that day. One of the adoption counselors at Helping Hands had a dog with three legs. She proudly exclaimed that her dog lived an active life and she saw no reason that Dixie could not do the same. Still, I hesitated. I asked if there had been any interest in Dixie. There had not. So I walked away, secure in knowing that she would be mine if I chose to listen to my heart.

Little got accomplished at work that afternoon. The welfare of the 100 or more children in my charge was always my priority but the mounds of paperwork I had set aside for the afternoon were nothing more than a pad for my elbows as I pondered the fate of this dog with three legs. It was time to consult my higher powers—Mom and the Early Education Center's assistant director (and fellow dog lover) Angie Gomez.

Angie and I had worked together for nearly three years. I was the captain of the good ship and crew while Angie was my first officer. The title hardly fit, as she was well versed in every aspect of center operation and could have run the place with one eye tied behind her back. Angie was also an outstanding teacher. She and her best friend Diane were greeting families at the door when the center opened 10 years before I arrived.

When it came to trading barbs, Angie could go toe to toe with anyone. During our six years together at the center, she hurled enough obscenities my way to make a sailor blush and I loved her for it.

Beneath the verbal horseplay, we respected one another professionally and a strong friendship developed that never strayed beyond the confines of the workplace. Contrary to popular belief, men and women can work effectively together without winding up in the sack or in court. We confided in one another about a variety of things.

So I talked to Angie that afternoon about this incredible dog I had met. I weighed the pros and cons of owning a dog in addition to being the single custodial parent of an 11 year old boy. Angie knew what was in my heart and rolled her eyes while I tried to be rational about it all.

"You have to get this dog," she said as she grabbed her coat and left for the day.

"When I find myself in times of trouble
Mother Mary comes to me
Speaking words of wisdom
Let it be . . ."

John Lennon/Paul McCartney, "Let It Be"

CHAPTER 5: BETTY JO

While Angie spoke for the right side of my brain, the occasionally rational and objective side was represented by one Betty Jo McHenry. She is known affectionately as "Jo" to friends and "BJ" to her family. To my younger sister Amy and me, she is just plain 'ol Mom.

Born in 1931 to a seamstress and Army veteran, my mother embodies all the positive qualities Tom Brokaw outlined in his book "The Greatest Generation." Mom and others like her endured the Great Depression, a world war, two wars in Southeast Asia, and the tumultuous 1960's. The latter might have been the truest test of her grit, as she and my father managed to raise two reasonably sane children in the midst of permissive parenting and recreational drug abuse.

I don't think I ever heard my mother say anything bad about anyone no matter how much she has been wronged over the years. She would give her shoes away in a blizzard if a friend asked. For her children she would sell her very soul. Her needs were always secondary to the family. Though my father was a good man in his own right, the same could not be said for him. They divorced after 40 years of marriage in 1993. We've never talked much about it but I suspect Mom didn't want to grow old with a man who was casually inattentive to her most basic of needs while never being tardy for tee time at the public golf course.

We lost Dad in 1997 well before his time. He was a man passionate about his kid's success. Dad wielded a heavy hand but made sure we had the best that his modest income could buy. Though we rarely stood on common ground, we grew closer after Josh was born in 1994. He was the best grandpa any kid could have. Sometimes I would watch him with Josh and not recognize the man who raised me.

My mom is humble to a fault. I thought she was going to stroke out when I threw her a surprise party for her 75th birthday. She is the proverbial worker bee. Let others make the decisions and lie around dreaming about what is to be. There is work to be done.

Mom was a medical secretary and transcriptionist at St. Francis Hospital for many years. At one time she could type more than 100 words per minute on a *manual* typewriter. She is a gifted writer but too shy for publication other than the occasional letter to the editor. Fiercely independent, I have caught her standing on a ladder pulling leaves and acorns from her gutters well into her seventies. Like many of her generation, you don't buy anything other than a house and a car unless you pay cash for it. This generation's obsession with unsecured credit baffles her to no end.

She was the kind of mom who finds a place to hang every kindergarten scribble brought home by an artistically obtuse son. My mom attended every one of Josh's soccer games on blustery spring days even though he rarely came anywhere near the ball. Her glass is always half full.

I came to Mom with the Dixie conundrum. First, she said, there were finances. I made a comfortable living as the director of the Early Education Center but was by no means living in the lap of luxury. With a dog there would be vet bills, food, and other pet supplies. The ASPCA estimates that the average household spends an average of $1,200 a year per pet. And let's not forget that pets are living longer these days thanks to advances in veterinary care. Would I be spending more to care for a dog with a disability? Are we looking at doggie physical therapy once a week for the next five years to rehab a dog with three legs? I hated being so pragmatic about adopting a living, loving, sentient being.

Then there was the time factor. Building a quality relationship with Dixie would mean exercising and training together. Would Dixie require more than the average dog? I was the single custodial parent of an 11 year old boy with Attention Deficit Hyperactive Disorder. I worked full time and was active in my church. I had family and friends stretching from British Columbia to just outside DC. Is having a dog going to keep me under house arrest for the next 15 years?

All valid concerns brought forward by Mom in a series of e-mails and phone conversations. She wasn't against the idea. Rather, she just wanted me to think it through. Just like my mom to be the agent of reality. Suddenly my heart was mute and Angie's words faded to black. Maybe this was more than I could fit on one plate. It was time to talk with Josh.

INSIGHTS: AM I GOING HOME TODAY?

One type of pain had been replaced with another. All I know is that I went to sleep on a table and my leg was gone when I woke up. Perhaps they sent it away to be fixed and I would get it back. Humans can repair almost anything. Now I hurt all over and my eyes were unable to focus. Walking took some getting used to and I stumbled a lot. People would take me to the yard to potty. Holding myself up so long made my right leg hurt. How was I ever going to catch a rabbit now?

Lots of kind people came to visit me. They smiled but I could smell the sadness on their breath. You can't fool dogs. Dogs can smell feelings in people so don't try to hide them from us. We know. I wondered if the man was going to take me home when a truck brought me back to the place with a million barking dogs. I walked in the building on my own while people cheered, then settled into my kennel for a morning snooze.

Suddenly there was a parade of humans staring at the kennels. The noise nearly split my ear drum then all was quiet as I locked my radar in on a solitary man ambling down the walkway. It was him. Not the man who delivered me here but the one that was going to take me home. I knew it the moment our eyes met.

"I am for you."

Somehow he seemed to know that. The next day, I went home—for good this time.

*"People smile and tell me I'm the lucky one
And we've just begun
I think I'm gonna have a son . . ."*

Kenny Loggins, "Danny's Song"

CHAPTER 6: THE LUCKY ONES

Yvonne and I have been separated since September of 1996. The divorce was final in May of 1997. I literally became a single custodial parent overnight. Custody was not contested. Even if it had been, I would have fought for that privilege. Yvonne got visitation every other weekend and was required to pay $200 per month in child support. Over time, she fell hopelessly behind with barely a reprimand from the courts.

Josh is an adopted child. Yvonne and I just weren't compatible when it came to procreation. She was not initially hip to "raising someone else's kid" but eventually warmed to the reality that adoption was our only viable option. We were approved by the State of Kansas as adoptive parents in July of 1993. In December of that year, we were informed that a teen mom had chosen us to raise her child from a host of other candidates.

Joshua Thomas McHenry was born on January 13, 1994. His parents were separated and well on their way to divorced by his third birthday. He lost his grandfather in November of his third year. Not exactly the way I had envisioned his life. In a word, 1997 sucked. The next nine years were spent raising a son and building a career. There was time for little else. Josh had an infectious smile, sparkling green eyes and dishwater blonde hair that bleached out in the summer. I think the term is "towhead." Despite struggles with ADHD, he managed to stay on the honor roll through his elementary school career.

My son was a gregarious little boy who never knew a stranger. It mattered not if it were human or canine. Josh was the preschooler who approached men standing at a public restroom urinal and announced that he and Dad were going to play miniature golf that day. In his innocence he knew no boundaries and I found his spirit to be infectious.

Josh was with his mother the day I had met Dixie at the shelter. I picked him up from school the following day anxious to tell him all about this amazing dog. Josh was intrigued by the idea of not only a dog but one with three legs. Mind you, this was the kid that would strike up a conversation with the child that others scorned. He missed Princess. After a failed marriage, an adopted dog was the closest thing to a sibling Josh was ever going to see. Obviously adoption was an easy sell. Josh and I had that in common. I was an adoptee as well. Now there was just one more inquiry to make.

I called Dr. Carder at Stonehouse Animal Hospital the day after talking to Josh. It had been 48 hours since I met Dixie on that magical October day. I simply could not shake the image of her head resting on my knee as we sat in that visitation room. He patiently answered each question from my list.

"Give her time to recover and then treat her like any other dog," he said, as our conversation came to a close.

Truer words, I have come to learn, have never been spoken and I have embraced them throughout Dixie's life.

"How much time will she need to fully recuperate?" I asked.

"I'd say about six months," Dr. Carder replied. "She will need time to build muscle mass in that front leg. Other than that, just love her."

Hell, I can do that. So could Josh. And the deal was sealed. I left work early and adopted Dixie just before the shelter closed.

You've heard this a hundred times if you are a champion of rescue dogs. We don't pick them. They pick us. But are we to believe that shelter dogs pass the dreary hours contemplating the qualities in a human that would be a good match for them? "Match.com/canine?" Or is it based on how dogs perceive the world? Dogs are incapable of expressing themselves through conventional language. They communicate visually and through their sophisticated olfactory sense.

How does the "right" person smell? What are the visual cues that tell a dog to move forward, look away, make eye contact, retreat, or to rest a cautious head on our foot in the visitation room? Is it not what we say with our bodies but how we say it that singles out one humanoid from another?

Somewhere in the top five of my bucket list is to be a dog for a day. Just a day. The whole butt smelling thing is difficult for me to fathom as a primate so I want some assurance that I can return to human form at the end of my day as a canine. Ah, but to perceive the world through the eyes and nose of a dog. How refreshing it would be to experience life uncomplicated by language and all of its hypocrisies and deceit. What a joy to give love at its most primal and pure. Now wouldn't that be something? What the hell, if I had to sniff a few posteriors in the process? When in Rome . . .

"Welcome to my happiness
You know it makes me smile
It pleases me to have you here
For just a little while . . ."

John Denver, *"Farewell Andromeda (Welcome to My Morning)*

CHAPTER 7: FINDING THE INNER DOG

Dixie was hurting despite the generous supply of Rimadyl sent home to manage pain. I had not noticed the extensive bruising before. A large purple mass blanketed one side or her torso like an ominous wall cloud that often accompanies a Kansas thunderstorm. It took Dixie no time at all to find a resting place on the couch. It was there that we would spend most of the next week.

Josh was not sure what to make of this new addition to our family. Grandma's dachshund Maggie would chase a squeaky soccer ball through the house as though she had been given intravenous injections of Red Bull®. Years ago, Princess had frolicked in the yard with us. But this dog just laid there. Her movements were arduous and she was not interested in the dog toys I had bought.

"The doctor said she would need some time to heal," I reminded Josh. "Just wait. You won't recognize her in a few weeks."

Patience was never one of Josh's virtues so he paid little attention to Dixie as she convalesced. There was something about this wounded animal that activated my nurturing gene. To this day, I believe that quality in me formed the bond that we share today. Little did I know that one day our roles would be reversed.

At the recommendation of the adoption counselors at Helping Hands, I arranged for a couple of days off work which would roll into a weekend just to be with Dixie. Josh was picked up from his after-school program on Friday by his mother so we had a four day weekend to lay the foundation of a beautiful friendship.

It was time well spent. Although the days were sunny and mild, I fought the urge to venture out other than for potty purposes or to catch up on some reading on the front porch. Dixie liked the porch after the sun had sufficiently warmed it up to her satisfaction. I watched as she took in the scents carried by a gentle fall breeze while lying prone at my side.

I spent the first three days and nights watching her every move. No one knew if she was potty trained so I was vigilant about taking her outside nearly every hour. I agonized with each lurch as she lumbered down the concrete steps that connected my porch to the sidewalk. Sometimes Dixie would relieve herself on the front lawn or the empty lot across the street. The house sat on an odd triangular lot so there was no back yard, per se. I figured the extra bit of walking would do her good.

Around 11 p.m. each night, I carted blankets and pillows from my upstairs bedroom so that I could sleep on the floor next to Dixie. My house was more than 80 years old and the staircase leading to the bedrooms Josh and I occupied was much too steep of an incline. While she learned to navigate most stairs with relative ease, it wasn't until a year later that she mastered the stairs in her own home. Unfortunately, it was a one way trip, as she was never comfortable coming down. Many days I would come home and find her marooned on the second floor.

There was a measure of connectedness that I felt lying next to this astonishing creature. Dixie would frequently moan in her sleep—a telltale sign that her medication was wearing off. I awoke to each sound much as I did when Josh was an infant. Parents understand that state of consciousness where you are sleeping soundly yet are acutely aware of your child's every sigh. This was how it was these first few nights with Dixie as we camped in the middle of my living room floor.

Dixie did manage to eat twice daily. I studied the feeding guidelines carefully on the bag of kibble, as Dr. Carder's warnings about excessive weight resonated each time I opened the pantry where the dog food was stored. She weighed 63 pounds. Dr. Carder felt her ideal weight was 60. Given her understandable lack of physical activity, I opted for ¾ cup in the morning and again in the evening. No snacks and certainly no table food.

Princess used to inhale her food as though it were the last bowl of sustenance left on the planet. Dixie was more deliberate. Her right front leg quivered as she strained to lower her head to the cheap plastic bowl. Though the reviews were mixed, I hustled out to PetSmart over the weekend and bought an elevated feeder. That seemed to help and slowly her enthusiasm for meals improved.

Our first official walk together took place on day three. It was warmer than usual for a late October afternoon in Kansas and Dixie was beginning to show some signs of life. I thought it best to begin with a jaunt around the block. Dixie sensed this was not a potty trip and seemed eager to test the waters as I attached her to a four foot lead. For the first time there was a spring in her step as though she had something special to show to the world.

I moseyed down the block at a casual pace. No problems so far. We headed up a small incline that connected the parallel streets. Dixie was panting noticeably by the time we reached the end of the next street. Her stride was no longer fluid and lacked that Tigger-like bounce that I observed on the way out the door. The sparkle, though, was still in her eyes. It was as if she was saying *"yeah, I can do this!"*

Dixie slept the rest of that afternoon. We took one of these walks per day for a week. By the end of the second week, we had graduated to a morning and evening walk. The tide was turning. Dixie was becoming a dog again. The indomitable spirit that has come to define this dog had taken hold.

"Follow me where I go
What I do and who I know
Make it part of you to be a part of me . . ."

John Denver, "Follow Me"

CHAPTER 8: POSTER GIRL

Josh had all but grown up in a community gathering place known as Gage Park. It was the backyard that I never had to mow. We could be found there nearly every weekend when Josh was younger and sometimes during the week when weather permitted. It was a massive spread spanning four city blocks in width. There was a public pool, a carousel, a mini train, a zoo, rose garden, and an arboretum. If that wasn't enough, there were numerous shelters and picnic areas, softball fields, an indoor and outdoor theater—even a horseshoe pit. And of course, playgrounds.

There was Josh pretending to be a pirate captain as he stood on the bow of a concrete ship. There he is again making friends as he scooped sand with a hand operated crane. Wait a minute, where did he go now? Oh, there he is—hanging out with another family and driving a wooden locomotive.

"Where are you going Josh," I would ask my then four year old son.

"Me and my friends are gonna go on a safari!" he gushed.

"Do your friends have names?"

"I dunno," he would shrug, and then disappear among the throngs of children all seemingly put there for his amusement.

Formal introductions took way too much time and required idle conversation. A friend was anyone who would indulge his vivid imagination. With all its amenities, Gage Park was the perfect launch pad for adventures worthy of a young boy.

Ironically, most of what made Topeka's Gage Park so engaging was there when I was a boy too. Little had changed in nearly 40 years. While I did not possess Josh's flair for the theatrical, I loved the zoo and was fascinated by the behavior of its residents.

One of the newest and brightest additions was the Bark Park. With some help from Hill's Pet Nutrition (a/k/a the Science Diet people), several dedicated volunteers converted a softball field into an off-leash area for dogs. The corporate offices for Hill's are based in downtown Topeka. It has been a terrific corporate citizen for many years. I was not surprised to find its logo plastered on the Bark Park signage. Its name is attached to several other community initiatives as well.

By now Dixie was up to three walks a day, and I began taking lunch breaks at home just to fit that third walk into our schedule. It was a 15 minute drive from the Early Education Center and Angie swore I was having a lunchtime rendezvous with a woman of questionable intentions. Partially true. I was lunching with a female but this was a lady of the finest kind. This was my Dixie. And it was time to introduce her to the world.

One Saturday morning, I told Josh we were going to Gage Park. By age 11, the park had lost some of its luster until I explained that we were taking Dixie to the Bark Park for the first time.

"Can we take a Frisbee®?" he asked.

All I could think of was stepping around little brown land mines to snag the wayward disc and wondered why Josh wanted to play there of all places. I hesitated so I could reply with something that didn't sound judgmental.

"I wanna teach Dixie to catch it in her mouth."

"Yea, right. We can do that," I replied with a tone of skepticism in my voice.

It was an unseasonably warm November day when the three of us set out for the Bark Park. So much so that Josh and I were in short sleeves along with many of the other patrons as we pulled into the parking lot. Josh grabbed the Frisbee® and left me to get Dixie out of the truck.

My pickup had a plastic bed liner that made traction difficult for a dog with three legs. Once free of the kennel, I reached gently around her girth and lowered her to the pavement. Dixie immediately caught the scent of other dogs and proceeded toward the entry with a sense of urgency I had yet to see at home. By the time Dixie passed through the gate, an impatient Josh had already cut loose with the Frisbee®. Dixie paid absolutely no attention to the airborne toy, preferring to sniff the genitalia of a Golden Retriever that had come to welcome her to the park.

Josh's shoulders slumped as he shot me a glance that implied an inherent flaw in this dog. With that, he hustled after the wayward disc intent on giving it another toss. I wondered who was training whom.

By now Dixie was fully engaged with the Retriever and I got to see the playful side of my once sullen adoptee. I was thrilled. The dogs exchanged play bows then would break into a cat and mouse game with each taking turns at being the pursuer. I had never really studied dogs at play before and found the nuances of the game to be quite captivating. In fact, I lost track of Josh all together. Apparently, he had been trying to toss the disc in Dixie's general direction and managed to procure the interest of every other dog in the park except for one.

Winded and frustrated by Dixie's indifference, Josh stood dejected at my side with the Frisbee® in hand.

"C'mon dude," I said. "There's plenty of room here for you and me to play. Dixie and her new friend won't even know we're on the other side of the park."

With that we spread across what was once the outfield of the softball diamond and tossed the disc back and forth as Dixie rediscovered her mojo. She seemed comfortable around other dogs and that was certainly a plus.

I had no idea what kind of celebrity Dixie would become. It was the same question everywhere we went.

"What happened to your dog?"

The story never got old. Reactions ranged from awestruck to "that poor doggie!" Dixie never consciously played the sympathy card which I suspect is the case with most dogs. Rather, her slap-happy gaze at the pity mongers seemed to imply:

"I'm fine, but there's something seriously wrong with your dog"

Sometimes children would want to see her run and Dixie was all too happy to oblige. On several occasions I told a group of kids that Dixie could beat any of them in a race. Invariably, one kid would step up and accept the challenge, then another. Dixie left each one in her wake and then came back for more.

Adults just marveled at her soulful eyes, plush golden coat and unwavering devotion to me. Then there were the inevitable questions. No, she wasn't born like this. Yes, she is adopted. No, she's not in any pain. Yes, she can run just like any other dog.

It started to get uncomfortable when people expressed their admiration of me for taking in such a dog as if it qualified me for sainthood. The perception seemed to be that Dixie was damaged goods and I had delivered her from a life of institutionalization or isolation in the bowels of some forgotten animal shelter. It certainly wasn't about me. Someone would have eventually adopted her and given her a wonderful life. I just happened to get there first. In fact, I preferred to deflect any praise lobbed in my direction.

"She has a fourth leg. I just left it at home." The comment was just irreverent enough to discourage further conversation.

No, I do not get the credit here. If anything, Dixie deserves the kudos for allowing me to become the center of her universe. I am incapable of that level of devotion yet she gives it to me freely each day.

Word of this amazing dog spread rapidly. Dixie was often the featured attraction at the off-leash park. Hikes seemed to take longer after Dixie joined the family. Even those visibly uncomfortable around dogs just couldn't help but take notice and offer an awkward scratch on the head.

In November of 2005, I received a call from Melissa Brunner, the local news anchor of the CBS affiliate in Topeka, WIBW-TV. Melissa was a board member of the local YWCA when I was employed as its youth services director. We served on a couple of committees together. Besides being a tireless advocate for victims of domestic violence, Melissa loved dogs and was scheduled to host a benefit for Helping Hands Humane Society called "Bone Appetite." Dixie and another dog were chosen as the honorary poster dogs for the spring 2006 event.

Melissa called and asked if she could produce our story that would be aired on an upcoming newscast. A longer version would then be viewed by the guests at the benefit later in the spring. I agreed and we met at my home over a lunch break. Melissa prompted me with a couple of questions and I told Dixie's story as I had done a hundred times before. I tossed a tennis ball her way and she actually chased it as though she knew she knew the cameras were rolling. Always the performer, Dixie the lab normally doesn't retrieve anything unless it can be consumed.

A week later, Melissa and a photo journalist met us at the Bark Park to shoot some additional footage. Melissa is a real pro and the segment was a gem. She graciously made me a copy that I have kept to this very day. My favorite part was when Dixie jumped up and kissed Josh squarely on the cheek. His reaction was priceless and reminded me of Lucy in the "Peanuts®" comic strip after Snoopy lays a big "SMAAAAAACK" on her face.

I couldn't have been more proud of Dixie as the clip ran on the big screen in front of a banquet hall full of Topeka's affluent. Ironically, Dixie had to stay at home, as the hotel would not allow pets inside. She did not have to be in attendance for her story to moisten the eyes of the faithful. It was truly magical.

"It's sad, so sad
Why can't we talk it over?
Always seems to me
That sorry seems to be the hardest word . . ."

Elton John/Bernie Taupin, *"Sorry Seems To Be The Hardest Word"*

CHAPTER 9: LIGHTNING STRIKES

While my relationship with Dixie continued to evolve, Josh and I were heading down a dark and dreary path. For reasons I never understood, children in the Topeka school system were promoted to middle school after completing the fifth grade. I didn't start what was then known as junior high until the seventh grade. Like most boys, I needed that extra year of seasoning at the elementary school level before I was mature enough to tackle the academic purgatory known as middle school/junior high. Josh was no exception.

Mom had told me for years that I was hard on Josh. My expectations were sometimes unrealistic. I often bristled at this notion but grew to accept it through some revelations in therapy with Josh. Despite my shortcomings as a parent, my son appeared to be a well-rounded kid with a bright future. Josh was enrolled in swim lessons. His teacher was impressed enough with his progress that she encouraged him to join a local swim team. Josh auditioned and made the local show choir. They had performed all over the city, including a gig with the Kansas Governor in attendance. Josh was active in the church youth group as well as their stage productions. He played flawlessly at his second piano recital. Sadly, his potential would never be realized.

Then along came middle school. Suddenly there were six different teachers, class changes, locker combinations, and eighth grade bullies. An outbreak of sexual experimentation forced teachers to take hourly peeks into bathroom stalls. Are you kidding me? Middle school? I had worked with children for many years and thought of myself as savvy to the ways of teens. Never did I think I would see a day where middle school students engaged in oral sex between classes.

The volume of homework was like nothing Josh had ever seen. His circuits overloaded and evenings at the dining table became a war zone. Josh stared into his text and I would nag. His chin would sink into his hands and I would rant. He shredded his paper when frustrated and I would scream venomous rants after reaching critical mass.

As Josh's middle school grades began to plunge, I enlisted the help of school officials who agreed that Josh was an intelligent boy. Too smart for any of the school's special services but not eligible for the gifted programs, Josh was simply dropped into the greatest chasm a child can fall into within the public school system. He was labeled an "underachiever." Simply put, the gap between his potential and his performance was growing by the day.

Concerned that he might be depressed, I enrolled Josh in counseling at the local guidance clinic. Josh detested the sessions and his contempt for me grew. My ex-wife thought it all a waste of time and participated in but one session and their mutual disdain did not go unnoticed. I sat quietly while the therapist probed and prodded but Josh was not forthcoming.

One day in a therapy session, the subject of my dad arose. Though only three when he died, Josh adored his grandpa and the feeling was mutual. The mention of his grandpa by the therapist triggered an emotional catharsis that led to more meaningful discussions. Perhaps we were making some headway. But the bliss was short lived.

It all came to a head in late November of 2005. Josh took a break from his homework and went out to get some air. He never came back. I paced. I called friends. No one had seen him. It was dark by now and I was frantic. Dixie and I walked the neighborhood. No Josh. I called the police to report Josh as a runaway. I called Yvonne and advised her of the situation. Then I headed to the police station to complete a runaway report.

I returned home and the phone rang. It was Yvonne. She claimed that Josh had walked to the public library (10 city blocks away) and called her. She and Josh met me at the police station. At the time I thought it odd that all this transpired after she learned that I had filed the runaway report.

For the first time in our 10 years together, Josh said he wanted to live with his mother. I told him that he needed to come home this evening and that we would talk about it. He skulked behind me and we rode home without speaking a word. And so it was for the next three days. A rift had come between us and we passed by one another like two ships in the night. I had never experienced such an eerie silence before in my home. What had I done?

Christmas 2005 was to be spent with my mother. Over the years, Josh had spent a considerable amount of time with Grandma and they had grown very close. Josh could do no wrong in the eyes of his very best friend and sometimes Mom had a difficult time picturing the increasingly angry child I often dealt with at home.

For reasons that elude me to this day, Josh did not want to celebrate Christmas with me or his grandma. He wanted to be with his mother. Custody over the holidays was always shared and this was my year but Josh would have none of it. He refused to get in the car when it came to leave for Mom's place. Determined not to cave to his demands, I left him at the house to ponder his behavior then sat dejected as Mom and I tried to make the best of a gift exchange. Josh's gifts remained unwrapped under the tree. Dixie's first Christmas in my home was anything but merry.

Josh was convinced that life would be better with his mom and he made that clear in the days following the Christmas debacle. Though it tore me apart inside, I knew in my heart that he needed to explore this possibility. I hoped he would discover that what makes the grass greener on the other side of the street is a lot of fertilizer. Like the prodigal son, I thought he would come home one day and we would symbolically kill the fatted calf in celebration.

In January of 2006, I let him go.

> *"He tried to tell us that the animals could speak*
> *And who knows? Perhaps they do*
> *How do you know they don't*
> *Just because they've never spoken to you? . . ."*
>
> Michael Murphy, "Boy From the Country"

CHAPTER 10: TEAMWORK

It was the spring of 1993. I enrolled Princess in a training class sponsored by Topeka Parks and Recreation. Once a week we met with approximately 20 other teams at a city park. We learned cues such as "sit," "down," "come," and "stay" as well as polite leash walking. For the first time I realized that training a dog was really about building a healthy relationship with a creature that is a species apart from my own. I had always loved Princess but training opened a window that allowed us to communicate in a way that I never thought possible. This notion was exhilarating and I took the training to heart. We practiced the cues daily per the suggestion of the trainer and Princess responded like a true Lab.

"Hey, this is fun! Was it good for you too? Great! Can we do it again? Huh? Huh? If it makes you happy, I'm happy!"

I was most impressed at her ability to sit automatically whenever I came to a stop. Most of our walking was done off leash so tethering her to me and watching her take cues from the movements of my body was absolutely fascinating. We eventually added "shake," "roll over" and "crawl" (as in military crawl) to the repertoire. I was ready for a guest shot on the Letterman show. "Stupid Pet Tricks," here we come.

Thirteen years later it was Dixie's turn. Carol Stubbs referred me to Rick and Perrin Riggs, two professional dog trainers who just happened to be husband and wife. We met at a local mall that actually allowed pets indoors. Like many malls, business was in decline. Many storefronts were empty and its walkways seemed more of an exercise venue for seniors.

Perrin did most of the talking while Rick silently observed and participated in some of the exercises. The Riggs volunteered their expertise to Helping Hands Humane Society in the form of a free training session. An additional four hours could be purchased for $80 and I cheerfully wrote a check after the freebie.

Perrin described herself as a positive dog trainer. This was a concept of which I was unfamiliar but would grow to embrace. Simply put, Dixie would be rewarded for performing cues correctly. The reward would be withdrawn for an incorrect response. No shouting or painful corrections. No choke chains or prong collars and certainly no electronic collars designed to administer an electric shock to "correct" a behavior. As a life-long pacifist, I was uncomfortable with the practice of coercing an animal (or anyone else for that matter) into compliance. The positive training that Perrin described fit right into my way of thinking. I wanted to know more.

Perrin introduced Dixie and me to a little device called a clicker. She explained that clickers and whistles had been used in the training of marine and circus animals for years and its purpose was to mark good behavior at the precise moment it occurs. Dixie sits and I click and give her a tasty treat as a reward. Dixie lies down and I click again and immediately follow up with a cookie. Makes sense although the coordination of cue, click, treat was a little like patting my head while simultaneously rubbing my stomach.

"This is gonna take some time," I thought.

Dixie was more than patient and clearly motivated by the presentation of food. That much I knew. This dog would eat a flavored rock if you put it in front of her and then come back for another.

As with Princess, Dixie learned several basic commands and our bond grew even stronger. She could not wait to train and her enthusiasm made it easy to set aside the time. I had more "down" time than ever now that

Josh was living with his mother and was unsure as to how to manage it productively. All the while, Dixie was helping me adjust to being alone by diving paws first into the training exercises given to us by Perrin and Rick. It was time to take a training class to see how she would perform around other dogs.

We began with an eight week PetSmart training class. Dixie could have quizzed out thanks to the Riggs but we stuck it out anyway despite an instructor that spent more time regaling us with tales of her home remodeling project than introducing techniques for teaching basic commands.

Dixie passed her beginning obedience course with ease so I decided to enroll her in a PetSmart intermediate class with a different trainer. He was a younger man with a shaggy beard and round wire frame glasses that bore a resemblance to John Lennon in his post-Beatle years. I pictured him sitting on the floor strumming a six string and singing "All We Need Are Dogs."

John (yes, his name really was John) was laid back and non-committal about most things. His placid demeanor nearly put me to sleep but seemed to have a calming effect on the dogs. Dixie learned to sit and lie down and stay with the "Three D's" known as distance duration, and distractions. We also learned "heel" and "stand" along with a few tricks such as "shake," "paw," and "roll over." With John's help I was able to communicate my wishes to Dixie even more effectively than with Princess. She complied as if she already knew what I wanted. I marveled at how quickly she picked up complex commands. It was like every essence of her being was bent on pleasing me. I did not deserve such devotion.

One particular command stands out as memorable for me and no doubt for Dixie. About midway through the intermediate class, John asked us to bring dog beds to class. The goal was to teach the dog to "park" or "go to your bed."

Dixie was all over this one. Her coveted bed was a large round stuffed thing that I picked up on clearance at PetSmart shortly after she came home with me. One side was plush while the other side was a slick synthetic of some type. I placed it on the floor and lured Dixie to bed with treat in hand. Dixie would follow a treat to the gates of hell so this one was a no-brainer. In a short time, I needed only to cue "go to your bed" followed by a point and Dixie parked on her carcass on the bed with the precision of a Maserati.

John instructed us to return with the beds the following week where we would add distance to the command. By that, we were to cue our dogs from several feet away. This proved a bit puzzling for Dixie at first, as she was more focused on the lure than the bed. I tried a more animated command, stepping forward from a distance of about five feet and Dixie promptly plopped herself atop the bed as if to say *"oh, that's what you meant!"*

John asked us to move the beds out of the classroom and into the store. Perhaps he wanted to see if the dogs would offer the behavior amidst the distractions of a pet store. Good call. I sat Dixie's bed near a free standing display of training products, backed away several feet and pointed to the bed.

Unknowingly, I had placed the slick side of the bed on the concrete floor. Dixie spun her wheels like a dragster at the starting gate (minus the smoke), built up a head of steam, and launched herself onto the bed like a tiger pouncing on its unsuspecting prey. The bed proceeded to slide across the floor with Dixie on board and slammed into the display, toppling it and spewing merchandise in all directions. In a panic induced frenzy, Dixie spun wildly in circles and barked at the steel display rack in what must have been a series of colorful metaphors. Store associates and trainer John came running to the source of the commotion only to break into hysterics at the crazy barking dog and a wrecked display. While outrageously funny at the time, it took me another month to get Dixie within ten feet of that damn bed. Eventually, her enthusiasm for the command returned and she now parks herself on it with great gusto.

Dixie passed her Intermediate class with honors and of course I was a proud papa. The bond between us had reached new heights and I was convinced as to the value of training. Dixie was learning how to live in my world while I was gaining insight into hers. The process of learning to communicate with her cultivated a relationship that would inspire the words on these pages.

Still, I missed my son and at times the yearning brought me to my knees. Going from a full time single dad to a weekend parent was a painful and often lonely transition but certainly made easier by the mere presence of an animal once described as "disposable." Was that her destiny? I mean, look at her name. Dixie. Dixie cups. Take a drink and throw it away. Not this dog. She was a keeper from day one and to this day I wondered if her previous owners regret letting her go.

Then there was my work. It was the second thing that defined me as a human being and gave me some sense of purpose. First, of course, was being a dad. But I was a father in name only by the spring of 2006. I immersed myself in the work while Dixie kept my head above the water.

> *"Take a look at me now*
> *Well, there's just an empty space*
> *And you coming back to me is against the odds*
> *And that's what I've got to face . . ."*
>
> Phil Collins, *"Against All Odds"*

CHAPTER 11: AN EMPTY SPACE

I imagined picking up a copy of the Saturday Evening Post at a newsstand. On the cover is a dark yellow Lab gazing out the front window of the living room keeping a silent but lonely vigil until her companion comes home. This was Dixie. I scattered toys and rawhides on the floor before leaving for work and found them in the same place and untouched upon my return. She would abstain from drinking on most days until I walked through the door. Norman Rockwell would have loved this dog.

Dixie's unwavering loyalty and devotion partially filled the enormous void created by the departure of my son. I never envisioned being a part time dad. Those who choose this role have been called "Disneyland Dads." Possessed by guilt, they treat their children to lavish gifts and vacations to exorcise the demon.

I was resolved not to become that in which I held in such disdain. Yet at the same time, I caught myself indulging Josh in activities I would have saved for special occasions during the days when he was with me full time. I so much wanted to remind him of the life he was missing in hopes that he would see the light and one day want to return. Our outings reminded me less of fatherhood and more of my time as a "Big Brother" volunteer. Show the kid a good time for a couple of hours and send him home. Despite Dixie's presence, the two-story, three-bedroom structure seemed cavernous, empty, and cold. My home had become a house.

One day there was an e-mail from Yvonne. When there was a bomb to drop, that's usually how it was communicated so my heart sunk like a rock whenever I saw my ex-wife's name highlighted in my "In box." Yvonne wanted to move to Arizona and take Josh with her. Her mother and younger sister still lived there and she felt disconnected from them. She went onto to say that the school system was better than what Topeka could offer. I could not have objected more adamantly as I had worked in Arizona as a case manager for nearly seven years. During the 80's, Arizona spent less money on its children than did Puerto Rico and there was little evidence to suggest that it had gotten better. Yvonne also claimed that my family was dispersed and that Josh would have a grandmother and an aunt close by.

I immediately called Josh to see what he wanted and he was understandably wavering. Although I knew he would miss me, he was most concerned about leaving my mother behind. He was far from decisive when I followed up a few days later but said he "thought" he would go with his mother to Arizona.

A tired scene plays out in almost every slapstick comedy filmed in the past twenty years. Some male character gets a whack to the groin. The audience laughs as though they had never witnessed this stich. Trust me when I tell you that it's nothing to snicker at. The excruciating pain paired with the sudden lack of breathable air makes you want to start following the little white light. Such was the feeling when I heard Josh say "I think I'll go with Mom."

In August of 2006, he was gone again, this time to Arizona. We spent our final weekend doing the things we had always loved—movies, a trip to a Kansas City amusement park, dinner at a gourmet burger joint, and a trip to the dog park with Dixie. Despite the carnival atmosphere, there was tension in the air. So many things to be said and yet any eye contact from me was deferred by a turn of the head. The hours counted down until it was time for me to return Josh to his mother's house. They were leaving the next day.

My eyes filled with tears as Josh said goodbye to Dixie. It was a poignant moment where dog and child sat nose to nose. No words were needed.

Josh tossed his luggage into the back of my pickup and we traveled north across the Kansas Avenue bridge. I looked upon my son's troubled 12 year old face while a song kept playing in my head like an I-Pod® in some sort of feedback loop. It was the song I sang to Josh minutes after he was born. I began to mumble the lyrics in a staccato choked back by a sadness that burned inside my throat.

> *"I don't want to walk without you, baby*
> *Walk without my arms about you, baby*
> *I thought the day you left me behind*
> *That I'd take a stroll and get you right off my mind . . ."*

It's an old song—some big band tune that was covered on a Barry Manilow album my mother owned. The tune was catchy and captured the essence of the first time I held my newborn miracle. Today the melody struck a melancholy chord. Then the dam broke and tears rolled freely down my face as I pulled into the drive. We hugged, I kissed him, and he walked away.

My body ached, my sinuses throbbed and my throat was raw as I lugged my 6'4" frame into the house. There was Dixie to meet me at the door just as she had done hundreds of times before. The tail wags but I am not smiling. The butt shakes and she begins to spin. It remains the ritual that precedes the afternoon walk. Her antics did not amuse me on this day. I collapsed into my oversized recliner with a fractured heart in my hands. Though no more than 1,200 square feet, the house was a corpse void of the lifeblood that once pumped through its veins.

It was time to reflect. Yvonne needed my permission to take him out of state. Rather than stand my ground, I deferred to a 12 year old when I knew that staying with me was the right choice. What was I thinking? I was the portrait of self-loathing. After sitting several minutes in silence, I eased myself down to the floor and lay beside my Dixie. Shamelessly I cried as tears trickled harmlessly onto her coat.

"What am I to do now? How could I have let him go again?"

I put on my game face at work. My teachers, being the astute observers of behavior that they were, knew something was not right in Denmark.

My shoulders slumped, my gait slowed, and my concentration waned. We often talked openly about our personal lives when time allowed. Angie knew as much about me as did my closest friends. You can't work in a pressure cooker with 130 children each day and not occasionally bend the ear of another associate. With boundaries in place, this type of support in the workplace can be invaluable and I encouraged it.

With Josh weighing heavily on my mind, I found that wearing the mantle of leadership at a large early education center left me exhausted at days end. All I wanted to do was fade into some mindless movie or sporting event and try to recharge the batteries. Dixie would have none of this. The remote device attached to the sun visor in my truck not only opened the garage door but was like a bark button to Dixie. It commenced within seconds after my right thumb left the steering wheel and found its way to the garage door opener. Once parked, I entered the house to a frenzy of drool and fur whirling counterclockwise like a figure skater's gold medal finale. This meant one thing;

"Geez I'm glad to see you now please get me the hell out of here 'cause I need to pee."

The jaunt across the street was more than just a potty break. It was the kickoff to our evening walk. My rendezvous with the Lazy Boy® had to wait. To keep it interesting for both of us, I varied the routes. My absolute favorite was a stroll through a charming little neighborhood known to the natives as "Potwin."

Potwin features some lovely colonial homes with an abundance of small town charm. It is particularly stunning in the fall with a combination of silver maples, oak, and birch trees blanketing the landscape with shade and color. Nearly every resident decorates with holiday lights and kids travel from all parts of the city to take part in the most generous Halloween giveaway ever. Halloween rivaled Christmas as Josh's favorite holiday of the year. The streets are cobblestone as are the sidewalks. There are still hitching posts at several street corners in the event someone needs to parallel park his Clydesdale.

The entire tour of Potwin covers a mile or so. Dixie was usually winded upon our return so we settle in for dinner. Kibble for Dixie and some frozen microwave entrée for me. It was no fun cooking for one. Dixie would curl up at my feet while I watched TV, read, or puttered around on the computer. I've never been a night owl, so I would head up the treacherously steep and narrow steps to my lonely perch around 11 p.m.

Weekends were another story. First and foremost, there was the Bark Park. Dixie made many friends here during our Topeka years. She has always been particularly fond of Golden Retrievers. While sociable and oozing with giddy playfulness, they are typically not bullies or overly rambunctious, which makes them the perfect companion for a dog with balance issues.

Dixie and I also enjoyed hiking trails. She remained on leash for the one shared by bikers and joggers. The other two were wooded and she was free to romp through the foliage. She was always most trustworthy in this regard and checked in at regular intervals to make sure I was keeping pace. Her front leg had grown quite strong, protruding from her shoulder like the trunk of an ancient sequoia tree. I marveled at her agility as she plowed through a trail while skillfully dodging divots, sharp objects and mud. Could it be that she knows how much I hate bringing a filthy dog into the cab of my truck, or did I have an emerging doggie diva on my hands?

Dixie's unselfish love was easing my transition into a more solitary lifestyle. It was late August of 2006 and I had already planned a visit to Arizona in the fall for my first stint as "Disneyland Daddy." This is the point where my life would be irrevocably changed.

"Yesterday
All my troubles seemed so far away
Now it looks as though they're here to stay
Oh, I believe in yesterday . . ."

John Lennon/Paul McCartney, "Yesterday"

CHAPTER 12: THE ACCUSATION

While spending a quiet lunch break with Dixie at home, I received a call from the priest at the church that housed my child care center. A seven year old girl claimed that I had taken indecent liberties with her in an empty meeting room during our after school care program. Although Father Pete O'Sullivan did not mention the child by name, I knew just who he was talking about.

Several months earlier, I had befriended a lonely little girl who was struggling to make friends in the after school program. She often sat alone with a book. To break the ice one day, I asked her to read a passage of her book aloud. She was clearly not a proficient reader. Occasionally I invited her back to my office where I had a collection of books behind my desk. "Alice" (obviously not her real name) would select a book and read it to me. The door to my office remained open throughout the day and was just a few feet from the main entrance.

Alice had come into my office to read on that day. When she finished, I walked her down a hallway towards the gym where the other children were playing. I had scheduled a seminar for my staff in a meeting room for later in the evening. As I walked Alice back to the gym, I decided to stop and see if the chairs and tables had been set up by the custodial staff of the church. Alice followed me inside. The chairs were stacked and the conference tables were leaning on their side against the wall so I opted to return and delegate the task to another staff member. Alice and I immediately left the classroom and resumed our walk towards the gym. The child's mother had just arrived to pick her up for the day and we met her in the hallway before reaching our destination. I exchanged pleasantries with the mother as I often did with arriving parents and returned to my office.

That was it. Somehow out of all that, the child reported to first her mother and subsequently to the school principal that I had assaulted her in that empty meeting room.

Father Pete explained that I was to be placed on administrative leave pending an investigation by the Police Department and Child Protective Services. He was apologetic and expressed confidence that all would be right again but he was obligated by law to report the incident and take these actions. I replied that I fully understood the drill and would comply. Angie was placed in charge of the center and I called to see if she was up to the task. Though outraged at the situation, Angie agreed to be the interim director.

I took the afternoon and pondered my fate. The Early Education Center had been rated among the top five providers in the area by virtue of a survey conducted by the local paper. Damage to the center's reputation would be irreparable if I were to remain on the payroll during the investigation despite my innocence. I could not permit this to happen.

After sharing my concerns with Angie by phone throughout the afternoon, I drafted a letter of resignation. The ship was not going down with its captain. I reasoned that putting some distance between myself and my employer, it might be possible to draw the scrutiny away from the center. I called Angie back and asked that she assemble the staff at Gage Park after work. All 18 associates were there when I arrived. There was not a dry eye by the time I had finished reading a prepared statement. I did not take any questions and walked away from my beloved staff for the last time.

My best friend for thirty years had been one Phil Smith. We were scheduled to have dinner that evening and I shared the gory details as we dined at a favorite Mexican restaurant. He was sympathetic and, as always, infinitely supportive but neither of us could have imagined the events that followed. After dinner, I drove to Father Pete's home and handed him my formal letter of resignation. He regretfully accepted it and thanked me for my service.

While running errands the next morning, I received a voice mail from detective Linquist (not his real name) of the Topeka Police Department. He asked me to meet him at the police station so that my story could be added to the investigation. I returned his call and we agreed on a 1 p.m. meeting time. Once I arrived, he took me to what I later learned was an interrogation room where we made small talk for several minutes. His initial questions were general in nature—who, what, when, and where. Then it got ugly. The detective stated that he had spoken with the child, he believed her story, and felt I was "hiding something."

It was like a parody from an episode of "CSI." Linquist would make up some lame excuse and leave the room. Unbeknownst to me, the interrogation was being videotaped for posterity. Apparently I was also covertly being observed by other detectives for any signs of discomfort and/or stress. They would find neither although the lag time between questions was nearly intolerable. There was nothing to do but sit and stare at a wall which had more personality than the detective had shown.

At one point, Linquist asked if I was a Christian. I was at the time and professed as much. He responded with something about eternal damnation if I didn't come clean. His ploys to bait me had become annoying.

"You're going to have to do better than that," I replied.

Another pause. Another departure. This egg would not crack and the detective had run out of provocations. I should have walked or refused to answer more questions without counsel but for some reason I stayed. Linquist returned again, leaned towards me, pounded his fists into the table that separated us in a vain attempt to intimidate me and called into question my manhood for not telling his truth.

I had nothing to add at this point so refused to justify the last comment with a response. Silence hung over the room like smoke in a seedy pool hall. Once more, detective Linquist left the room. I later learned that I was his first interrogation, as he had only been promoted to the rank of detective just two weeks prior. No doubt he exited to be coached by a superior but to no avail. The truth was before him. I had done nothing wrong. In the absence of any evidence or witnesses, a child's statement became police exhibit number one. Detective Linquist returned to the room and informed me that I was being arrested for taking indecent liberties with a child. I showed no emotion which seemed to trouble Linquist. He asked why I wasn't visibly angry or tempted to reach over the table and rearrange his face.

"You really don't know me very well," I said and turned away.

I remained stoic, not wanting to give anyone the satisfaction of seeing a defeated man. A million thoughts bombarded my consciousness as my world crumbled around me. Then my attention turned to Dixie. Who is going to take care of Dixie?

A uniformed officer returned to the interrogation room and asked me to put my arms behind my back as he checked for weapons. Finding none, I heard the snapping of handcuffs and the sensation of unforgiving metal against the bones in my wrists. I was led to a squad car. The back seat was cramped and I leaned in awkwardly with help from the officer. It's not easy getting in or out of a car without the use of your hands.

Several minutes later, the squad car pulled into the garage of the county jail. I was escorted through two secure doors and into a lobby to be processed. My pockets were emptied of all belongings. Each item was carefully inventoried and placed in a bag. Fingerprints were taken and I was placed behind a camera for mug shots.

A few months back, I had received a call that began with a recording.

"This is a collect call from the Shawnee County Jail. Press one to accept, two to decline."

Those may not be the exact words but it was something to that effect. I was curious so I took the call. It was from a guy I went to school with who had been in trouble most of his life. We had bumped into one another weeks before at a department store and chatted for a few minutes. It was an uncomfortable conversation, as this person was a bully and I was often the recipient of his torment. As we spoke, I noted that he was much smaller than I and how much fun it would be now to exact some much deserved revenge. At any rate, he was in trouble again and was reaching out to anyone that might be able to bail him out of jail. I could not accommodate him so the conversation ended quickly.

Now it was my turn to make that call. Naturally, I called Mom. She picked up the phone and that dreadful recording kicked in before I could utter a word. Her voice expressed alarm so I tried to remain calm as I explained my situation. My mother, normally as cool under fire as they come, broke down as I tried to maintain my own composure. It was the Friday evening before the Labor Day weekend. There were no lawyers to be found and neither of us knew what to do next. Mom said she would call our pastor, Rev. Jim McCollough, as well as best friend Phil for advice. For the time being, I was a prisoner in the jail for what might be several days due to the holiday. This prospect suddenly became all too real. Mom said she loved me. It was a sentiment that she did not express often but it was what I needed to hear at that moment.

In the movies, the accused is always given one phone call. I was given two. The second call was to Angie. The recording kicked in again and I tried to talk over it before she hung up thinking it was another one of my pranks. It must have worked because she accepted the call. I repeated what I had told Mom and asked if she would be willing to keep Dixie. Angie choked back some tears and agreed. Mom had a key to my house so I asked that she call and arrange to meet somewhere.

"Please take care of my dog."

And I hung up the phone.

I was escorted to a holding cell to await a medical examination. It was a room void of any warmth with only a bench for comfort. Though dinner time had come and gone I was not hungry. My world had grown dark and I curled up on the unforgiving bench a broken man. A nurse came in and took my blood pressure and pulse. She asked if I was suicidal. I did not reply, so she asked the question again with more urgency in her voice. I replied that I was not but the notion seemed strangely compelling at that point.

A couple of hours passed before I was taken to another room to be processed into the county jail's living quarters. Once assigned to a cell block, I was unceremoniously handed prison garb and told to remove my clothing for a body cavity check. The indignity of the moment was lost as my senses went numb from the entire ordeal. I was awake but in a stupor as if my mind and body were slowly beginning to shut down.

The jailer led me down a maze of corridors and delivered me to the cell block. There was a commons area with tables that reminded me of a school cafeteria. Cells blocks housing several inmates surrounded the open area. Each cell block had several bunks and two toilets separated only by a partition. I was given a small pillow and a blanket for the bed. Once settled, I was offered dinner but refused. Prisoners moved about freely during what was a recreational period. Most chatted at the tables. Others wandered around aimlessly. A slightly built man asked me if I was going to eat whatever they had put on my tray. I shook my head and he helped himself, pulling the tray away from me as if he were a lion tearing at raw flesh after a kill. Welcome to the jungle.

Before retreating to my cell, I asked a guard if he knew when my initial hearing was scheduled. He replied that it could be mid-week due to the holiday. With that bit of good news, the reality of the next few days became clear. I was a prisoner at the Shawnee County Jail and I wasn't going anywhere for several days. There was nothing to watch, nothing to read, no one to talk to. I collapsed in my bunk around 9 p.m. An hour later, the cell doors closed automatically to a hollow clang as the latching mechanism secured. I gazed into a single cinderblock as the hours passed, interrupted only by the snoring of the other inmates.

The door to the cell block automatically opened around 7 a.m. Inmates staggered out into the commons anticipating a morning meal. Food was the last thing on my mind but I sat at the table like everyone else for lack of anything better to do. No sooner than a plate of scrambled eggs and toast was placed before me did the same wispy man approach and again asked if I wanted my food. I just shook my head and the entire tray was gone in the wink of an eye. After thirty minutes, we were sent back to our cell blocks so that the cafeteria personnel could clean up after the meal.

The automatic doors glided to a close, then re-opened shortly after for a recreational period.

I trolled about the commons area, growing more depressed by the hour. Three men were in a makeshift gym playing basketball and I wandered over thinking some exercise might pass the time. A ball rolled past me a couple of times and I picked it up and launched a shot from about 15 feet away. Air ball. I took another shot with the same result. Some laughter followed and I could feel the rush of blood to my face and I headed toward some stairs leading to the second level of cellblocks. Once to the top, I leaned out over the railing and contemplated the bleakness of my situation.

So this is jail. How long would I be stuck here? Could my mother, friends, and colleagues carry the cross of my shame if I were to be convicted of this lie? Would I ever see Josh or Dixie again? I had never felt so alone. I considered the extent of my injuries if I were to fling myself over the railing to the floor below. If I were to do a swan dive I could land on my head and death would be instantaneous. Or perhaps aiming for a table could sufficiently sever my spinal column at the neck. No sense lingering around in a body cast. Paralysis is just another kind of prison. The only question was whether I was high enough to end this nightmare.

Is it courage or cowardice that finally convinces a man to end his life? Maybe a bit of both. Either way, I was ready. Just then a guard took notice of my precarious lean over the railing and yelled up at me to come down. The other inmates caught the sense of urgency in his voice and turned to see what all the commotion was about. I paused, somewhat embarrassed by the attention. Slowly, I withdrew from the railing and walked back down the stairs to the commons area. The guard called me over to his work station and asked if I was wanted to hurt myself. I lowered my head and retreated back to my bunk without answering. It really didn't matter anymore. The first guard mumbled something to his partner and I later learned that I was on a suicide watch. I napped for a time and was awakened for a lunch I had no intention of eating.

INSIGHTS: WHERE ARE YOU?

Something was wrong. The hour was late and Tim was not home. Humans mark the passing of time by staring at their wrist or checking their phones. Dogs just know. We study your habits. I'll bet you didn't know that about us. All I know is that Tim never comes home after the house gets dark. Yes, something was definitely wrong.

I was sleeping and woke to headlights shining through the window. It was a car. They used to terrify me. Now I have come to accept them since Tim started giving me treats whenever we stopped at the place where cars come together to discuss their diabolical plan for ridding the world of dogs.

I barked at the light and heard the voices of people approaching the house. One was a child. They smell sweeter than adults and are usually not covered with foul smelling fragrances. The front door began to open and I felt the fur standing up on my back. I barked a warning but relaxed when I heard my name. The light came on and I could see that it was a woman and a little girl. I did not know the child but recognized the scent of the adult. It was one of the people who Tim worked with but what were she and the child doing in our house? Where was Tim?

Smelling the fingers of the little girl reminded me of Josh. He was special to Tim so he became my friend too. On nights where Tim and Josh watched the images on the big screen, Josh would sit on the floor and hand me the crust from his pizza. I would sit for hours drooling for just one more bite of that chewy stuff. If Josh was tired, we would lay down together and he rested his head on my ribs. Josh talked to me and we played chase at the dog park. I missed Josh but it was a lot quieter around the house now. Josh and Tim used to bark at each other a lot and it wasn't because they wanted to play a game. These were angry barks and I could feel the love in their hearts being smothered by something very dark and dreary.

I recognized the lady. Her name was Angie. She and the girl led me away to their house where I would stay until it was light again. This made no sense to me and I ran along the fence in the backyard trying to find a way to get to Tim. He needed me now more than ever. He needed me the way I needed him when my injured leg dangled helplessly from my body.

I stayed with Angie and her family overnight and into the next day. They were so very kind to me but I missed my home. Tim was nowhere to be found. I was so worried about him that I ignored the food Angie put in a bowl. She eventually got out some food from a can and the aroma reminded me that I had not eaten since the morning.

The girl's name was Madison. She fed me from the table when her mother wasn't looking so I followed her around the house all evening. Later I rested at the foot of her bed as she slept. I waited all night for the opening of the garage door that signaled Tim's arrival. The hours passed and still he did not come for me. Where could he be?

Daylight finally arrived and I discovered that there was a dog park behind Angie's house and I had it all to myself. Dog parks are more fun when there are other dogs around but there were plenty of interesting smells to occupy the moment. Angie put some more canned food in a bowl but I was not hungry. By now I was way past worried. I was frantic and paced the house. Angie thought I needed to potty so let me back into the dog park. I paced the fence, stopping only to stare down a passing car hoping each just one would pull into the drive long enough for Tim to get out. I was alone again and the only thing missing was that old tie down.

*"I was bruised and battered I couldn't tell what I felt
I was unrecognizable to myself
I saw my reflection in a window I didn't know my own face
Oh brother are you gonna leave me wastin' away?"*

Bruce Springsteen, "Streets of Philadelphia"

CHAPTER 13: MISSING IN ACTION

His name was Tom and he was charged with domestic violence. We met at the lunch table. I did not give him my name nor did I tell him what I was accused of and thankfully he didn't ask. Apparently he and his wife had gotten into some sort of an altercation. Tom pushed her in the heat of the moment and the police were called. By statute, the perpetrator of any sort of domestic violence complaint is arrested at the scene. Tom seemed remorseful and as terrified by his predicament as I was. We must have seemed quite out of place to the other inmates, some of whom I overheard swapping stories of their multiple incarcerations.

Tom had people working on the outside to post his bail and expected to be released at any time. He seemed to be a decent guy, a salesman by trade. Nothing like some of the other thugs I had been forced to share close quarters with. He talked of his children and the rocky marriage he hoped to reconcile. Listening to his story temporarily took my mind off my woes so I was eager to offer a friendly ear. The guard said that a cart with books would be around on Tuesday. It was Saturday and there was nothing to do. It was as if someone replaced the sand in the hour glass with gravel.

Tom and I, or rather Tom, must have talked for two hours. I overheard someone say it was fast approaching 3 p.m. I had been jailed for nearly 24 hours. A guard approached the cell where Tom and I had settled in. He called my name and said "you're free—someone posted your bail." I glanced sympathetically at Tom and wished him well but wasted no time getting the hell out of there.

A bailiff escorted me through a maze of hallways to a small room where my clothing and personal effects were stored. I quickly signed for what was mine and was led back to the lobby where this dreadful nightmare had begun.

There was my Phil, my best friend since my college days. He was smiling as though he were picking me up for a movie. A man was standing next to him. We embraced as we always did and I was introduced to a bail bondsman. Somehow Phil, my mother and Rev. McCollough had managed to connect with this individual and make arrangements for my bail. Apparently it was set at $10,000 and my guardian angels had managed to come up with the necessary deposit to spring me. I signed some paperwork and climbed into Phil's Toyota minivan.

As I eased into the seat, it suddenly dawned on me as to just how emotionally exhausted I was. I had not eaten in two days. Worst of all, I was ashamed and could not look at my son's godfather and the best man at my wedding. We had experienced both elation and despair over a 25 year friendship but nothing like this. Phil knew something was wrong and his mood sobered. He asked if I was hungry. I shook my head as I gazed out the window at nothing in particular and mumbled that I could use something to drink. Phil stopped at a convenience store. My stomach was bubbling, so I grabbed a clear soda in hopes of calming the rush of acid churning in my belly that was signaling a hunger I could not recognize.

"Where to you want to go?" Phil asked sympathetically.

"Home," I said without taking my eyes off the window.

Phil paused to see if I would make eye contact.

"Why don't we check in with your mom first."

I nodded and we arrived at my mother's house 10 minutes later. She hugged me as I stepped through the door. Mom is not an overly affectionate person. Hugs were rare in our home. It was a form of expression reserved for holidays and prior to long departures. She threw a troubled glance at Phil who replied with a shrug and a shake of the head. I was not the same person they knew nor would I ever be again.

Mom's embraces always triggered a rush of emotion, perhaps due to their infrequency, their intensity, or both. This was no different and what energy I had left to maintain a sober exterior imploded and I cried like a little boy on my mother's shoulders as my knees began to buckle.

Mom and I both love tennis. I play while she prefers to watch. The US Open was on TV as I sat down on the couch. She and Phil were mumbling in the next room, no doubt about my zombie-like appearance. I watched curiously as she handed him a check, thanked him profusely, and embraced him with more gusto than she had with me just moments before. I waved dispassionately and thanked Phil with all the sincerity I could muster though I wasn't exactly sure what had just transpired.

Dixie! Where was Dixie? Suddenly I was awakened from my catatonic state wondering if Angie had picked her up from my house. Mom assured me that Angie had been keeping Dixie at her place. All I could think of at that point was being reunited with my dog.

First things first: To get Dixie, I had to find my truck. I had parked in the police station lot before going in for my interview-turned interrogation with Linquist. The need for sleep and something edible to soothe my restless stomach was secondary now as I asked Mom for a ride downtown to retrieve the vehicle. She offered food but I declined and asked that we leave straight away.

My silver Toyota pickup was still parked where I had left it at the police station. Climbing in the cab felt like putting on a favorite pair of jeans. Something familiar felt strangely comforting for a fleeting moment. The engine turned over and I was on my way to Angie's house to get my beloved Dixie dog.

I rang the bell and Angie opened the door. Her eyes spoke volumes before she said a word. She looked me over from head to toe, seemingly taken aback by my feeble appearance.

"You look like crap," she said.

The comment elicited a faint smile. Angie was not one to hold anything back, especially where I was concerned. I loved her frankness. She had that unique ability to instantly and accurately cut to the chase which made her invaluable as an assistant, and, not to mention, as a friend.

Angie's rambunctious Shepherd came bounding up the stairs from the family room with Dixie in tow. She leaped on me with her front leg pointing skyward as though she were trying to comb my disheveled hair. She spun in circles, tried to impress me with a sit but was so fidgety that she nearly capsized. Dixie missed me. Angie insisted that Dixie was no problem and her children loved having another dog to play with. Still, caring for my dog in an emergency was one of the greatest acts of friendship ever bestowed upon me and I told her as much. We embraced, perhaps for the first time. Angie never was the touchy-feely type.

The kennel seemed unusually heavy so Angie helped me load it into the bed of the truck. I figured the bag of food inside accounted for the extra weight and didn't think anything of it. All that mattered now was that Dixie and I were reunited. At that moment, I knew I never wanted to be apart from her again.

I drove back to Mom's house and tried to watch tennis but it was as if I was looking at the screen through a magnifying glass. I could see images but was too preoccupied to focus on their movements. Dixie rested at my side as I eased back the recliner and tried to sleep. Even the slightest move on my part prompted a quick gaze from her prone position on the floor. It was like she was saying *"are you OK?"* I was not.

Mom offered food but my stomach was upset and I politely declined. She could not hide the worry lines on her face as she returned to the kitchen with the food barely touched. This scene would repeat three times a day over the next two weeks. I had no appetite. The association with food, especially when shared with family and friends, had always been a joyful one and for the first time in my life the mere sight of it turned my stomach. After two weeks with Mom, I had lost 30 pounds and was unrecognizable even to the face in the mirror. That gaunt face must surely belong to someone else. Mom had stopped eating too.

Nights were the worst. For days I tossed and turned. My mind raced with scenarios of my life playing out behind some prison wall. My gut twisted with recollections of an awful mug shot that aired on all three local television stations. There were articles in the local paper followed by hateful on-line postings so vile that I eventually stopped reading them. Peace could not even be found in sleep, as my dreams took me to places my conscious mind dared not go.

Perspiration lined my brow as I awakened in a dark room to a racing heart and throbbing pulse. Unable to get back to sleep, I would retreat to the living room recliner and stare mindlessly into the night. As the muscles in my stomach knotted, I lowered myself to the floor to curl up with Dixie who had left the comfort of our bed to be at my side. Stroking her velvet coat and looking into her softened eyes was calming despite the vat of acid brewing inside my stomach. Lying in a fetal position pressed up against my dog was the only peace I could find and Dixie apparently had nowhere else to go at 3 a.m. Sometimes I would drift off but for no more than thirty minutes. One stomach cramp later and my eyes were open and fixated at the ceiling with Dixie's head resting on my shoulder. Her sleep was intermittent as well. Each time I awoke, my eyes met that gentle face and I knew the dawn of another day was approaching but the nightmare that had become my life continued

Upon my release I learned that I was to meet weekly with a probation officer that would monitor my behavior for an undetermined amount of time. The mere fact that I had been assigned to this person led me to think that the system had already determined my fate. The conditions of my newfound freedom were made clear. I could not leave the state. I could not be in the company of children and I certainly couldn't take a job that involved caring for them. The probation officer was firm but pleasant and I was nothing if not respectful in return. I told her of my plans to visit Josh in the spring. She contacted the judge and the travel restriction was waived. I could see Josh but he was not to spend the night with me.

If there were questions as to whether I would need an attorney upon the initial contact from local police, all doubts had been erased now. Many parents of the children we once cared for called or wrote with messages of love and support. One recommended Don Hoffman, a veteran trial lawyer who had represented their family business for many years. I called Don on Tuesday following the Labor Day weekend. He had read about my arrest in the paper and invited me to meet him within the hour. Mom wanted to go as well and I welcomed her support. I quickly showered and we hustled downtown to an office several floors up a bank tower.

I was told that Don was an outstanding trial lawyer. He was known as a tiger in the courtroom and had a reputation for intimidating young prosecuting attorneys. In fact, Don was described by more than one person as being an jerk at times but a guy you definitely wanted in your corner. I learned very quickly that Don was forthright, brazen, deliberate, and brilliant.

Don required a $3,000 retainer which Mom ponied up without reservation. We discussed little of the case details in our initial meeting. Don was just getting a read on me. He quickly concluded that I had been emotionally traumatized by the recent events and set up a second meeting to piece the puzzle of this accusation together. At that point, he said the one thing that gave me a reason to smile for the first time in days. He believed me. I had me an attorney.

Don introduced me to his legal assistant, an engaging 50-something woman with snowy white hair named Jane Laptad. Jane was an enigma unlike any woman I had ever met. It was Jane's job to provide Don with the details to build my case and we began meeting weekly. Ultimately, Jane's tireless work on my behalf saved me thousands of dollars (legal assistants work cheaper than trial lawyers).

I returned home feeling better than I had in days. It occurred to me that Dixie had not been on a walk since I landed at Mom's place. Had I been so neglectful in the past, I would have felt a chilled proboscis pushing my forearm skyward. Dixie was hardly subtle when it came to reminders that there were scents to be marked and neighbors to be greeted. Most of the first week at Mom's I had spent prone on the couch. Dixie never ventured far, maintaining a silent vigil in hopes that I might one day make grab for the leash.

One day I did just that but was overcome with panic. What if someone saw me? My face had been splashed all over the electronic and print media. I had worked in highly visible non-profit circles in Topeka for 16 years. By no means was I a celebrity but I had done radio public service announcements, been interviewed on TV and had been quoted in the local paper on several occasions. The scenario played out in my mind again and again.

"There he is—there's that guy. The one they arrested for molesting that child!"

I could see it all; the looks of disdain, the hushed whispers, the subtle finger pointing. Dixie's leash hung from the door knob for several more days. It took all the courage I could muster just to take her out in the yard and sit in the shade while she sniffed at the same shrubs before collapsing in a heap next to my lawn chair. No doubt she yearned for the active life we once enjoyed. Anxiety induced tremors riddled my body every time I entertained the notion of going outside. Mom insisted we take the occasional car ride to my house to pick up whatever essentials I would need to remain under her watchful eye and I dreaded each one.

There were notes attached to my door from the media offering opportunities to disclose "my side of the story." Everyone wanted a scoop. The world was closing in on me and flight mode had kicked in. What if I took Dixie for a walk and just kept going? Surely my birth family in British Columbia would welcome me with open arms. Getting across the border didn't require a passport in 2006 but it soon would. I sent an e-mail to my birth mom and sister Sherri. The reply was cool at best and not what I expected. I needed options. Dixie still needed a walk.

It never occurred to me to invite Mom on a dog walk. Dixie and I had taken many walks around Mom's neighborhood in the past but never once did she accompany us. Mom is not the type to go much out of her comfort zone. I was a senior in high school before I ventured more than 100 miles from Topeka. She took walks in the mornings with a neighbor so was not opposed to putting feet to pavement. I just never bothered to ask for her company figuring she would politely decline because of some impending rendezvous with the dishwasher. Today I asked and she readily accepted. It was to be the first and only time.

Dixie had been disconnected from her leash since my release from the Shawnee County Jail two weeks prior. It was an unseasonably warm evening for September. It wasn't long before I could feel the perspiration on my brow and noticed that the left side of Dixie's face had been soaked by a tongue dangling out the side of her mouth like a flag in a stiff breeze. I felt the muscles in my legs tighten after a block. I had been jogging or riding my bike almost daily for years in addition to walking Dixie and thought myself to be in decent shape but weeks of inactivity had left me withered and weak.

People throughout the neighborhood were quietly going about their business. I kept my head down, careful to avoid eye contact with anyone. My stomach was doing somersaults and the burn of anxiety filled my chest. I had to get back to the house. These people were all looking at me. To make matters worse, I was walking a three-legged dog that always drew attention. I once joked that a fringe benefit to being a companion to Dixie was the potential for meeting attractive women that took pity on her. Today the prospect of being approached by anyone sent me to a place I had never been before. I had heard about anxiety attacks but blithely dismissed them as a symptom of mental illness to which I had thus far been immune. Mom and I headed home after fifteen minutes. My heart was racing. Not from the exercise but from being out of my cocoon that took the form of the tiny house on Bowman Court.

I did not sleep the night following that first walk and many nights after that. My mind was flooded with worst-case scenarios. Police, the media, more jail time. This thing had taken on a life of its own and I was no longer in control of anything. It reminded me of a time I went white water rafting in Arizona. Our small boat managed to capsize and I was whisked away by the current. My life jacket kept my head well above the waters of the Little Colorado but the river owned my body. After being thrashed about the rocks for several minutes, I managed to crawl back into the boat as the waves subsided. What a terrifying prospect it is to lose control over any aspect of your life, let alone *every* aspect of it. The river had me again and this time there was no vest to keep me afloat and no boat to rescue me.

Weeks passed and I had heard nothing from the district attorney's office as to whether a charge would be filed, and little more from Don. Meanwhile Child Protective Services informed me that the case had been "substantiated." Simply put, I was guilty based on interviews with the child and supposedly other witnesses. Angie said she and several teachers at the Early Education Center had been interviewed as well as some parents and that all were steadfastly supportive. The Court of Child Protective Services was not constitutionally bound to view me as innocent until proven guilty. Children never lie and this was a slam dunk from their perspective. Still, no word from the DA. Don didn't seem to see this as a setback. I sunk further into the well.

I had been unemployed for three weeks. Despite Mom's benevolence and endless hospitality, my bank account was all but drained and I needed to work. Phil was an insurance claims adjuster specializing in property damage and asked if I wanted to be Robin to his Batman. I agreed and we spent the latter part of September and October climbing roofs and assessing hail damage. It was treacherous work at times, as we were often two and three stories above the ground on an incline that tested my faith in gravity. Truth be told, Phil did all the assessing. I held the tape measure, carried the ladder, jotted down measurements, and drove the service vehicle so he could return calls or catch a wink or two between jobs. In exchange, Phil paid me what he could and always bought lunch. He insisted on banter while we drove even though my thoughts were a million miles away.

Phil seemed to know when my mind was taking me to a darker place. No one laughs like Phil. It ranges from a robust ho-ho-ho emanating somewhere between his navel and his kneecaps and rises in pitch until it crescendos into a falsetto. He laughs at everything. That's the way I picture him leaving this world. I used to make him laugh all the time. But I was anything but funny now. Still, he managed to keep things light as we traveled all over eastern Kansas and western Missouri. He proved to be a friend like no other.

On more than one occasion I stared into the abyss from the top of a building and secretly wished that I would fall. It would look like an accident and this nightmare would finally be over. But what if Josh wanted to come home? What if Mom's health failed and she needed me? Who would take care of Dixie? Commuting from Topeka was putting 140 miles per day on my car but I was so thankful for the work. Not only could I pay the mortgage on the house (with Mom's help) but I felt liberated and almost human in a different city where no one knew my name or my story. Even though it was front page news in the local paper, the Kansas City media apparently had little interest. There were some nights that we didn't finish roof hopping until sunset and Phil offered me a spare bedroom if I was too tired to drive. Occasionally I took him up on it. One day I asked if I could rent the room until I had saved enough money to get an apartment. He talked it over with his wife Barb and the kids. It was agreed.

I left some clothes at Mom's and took what I needed to Phil's four bedroom suburban home. His two children, Jenny and Justin, loved Dixie and she them. The Smith family shared a home with two Golden Retrievers. There was rumbling, bumbling, stumbling Cody, and Katie, a diva with selective tastes in most everything. One more animal in the house was probably less of an intrusion than having me around. When not working with Phil, I retreated to the safety of the guest bedroom where I could read or watch TV in relative calm.

Dixie loved to play with Cody and Katie. The trio soon became back yard hellions. Best of all, Dixie was always tired when I got home. I had always been close to Phil's children. But kids terrified me now and I spent the evening secluded in my little room upstairs. Occasionally Justin and a neighbor chum would knock and I would make up any excuse to shoo them away. The guy once known as the Pied Piper to children no longer had a tune to play.

INSIGHTS: "I AM FOR YOU"

Grandma's house smelled like sadness. The scent consumed Tim and was very evident in Grandma as well. There was no laughter and Tim seldom spoke above a whisper. For hours he would lay on the couch. I sensed that he needed me close so I curled up on the floor beside him. The sun was out and the air felt cool. It was the kind of day where we would hike or maybe go to the big dog park. I so much wanted to be outdoors but knew that Tim needed me right where I was. There were times where Tim did not come home at night and I became part of the sadness. Patiently I would wait by the front window, alerted only by the slamming of a car door. When I discovered that the sound came from across the street, I sighed and returned to my post. Tim would pass through a nearby portal soon and I wanted to be the first thing he would see.

I could barely contain myself when Tim's truck pulled into Grandma's driveway. At our house he would greet me in a high pitched "Dixie-Dooooooo!" I had not heard this tone since we began sleeping at Grandma's house. The light in his eyes had dimmed. His skin was pale and he smelled sickly. Even so, he seemed glad to see me and I spun around several times so he would know that I missed him too. In my heart I knew he would always come back for me.

I liked Grandma. She was an older woman who Tim and Josh loved very much. Grandma's house always smelled like food so I was happy to be there. Canine moms lose interest in their children after a time but human moms never do. I am envious of humans in that way. Sometimes I miss the sparkling yellow dog that was my mother and wonder what became of her and the puppies that made up our family.

Maggie is a pudgy little dachshund. She was for Grandma. I liked Maggie too. She would carry a small squeaky ball in her mouth, drop it in front of humans and whine until they tossed it. Despite my heritage, I never cared to retrieve anything I couldn't swallow, so Maggie's game made no sense to me. Still, it was fun to watch those little feet scamper along the floor, settle under the ball, and catch it her mouth. This made Grandma smile and it seemed that smiles were in short supply.

When Josh was around, we used to take a ride in the car and visit Tim's best friend Phil and his family. Like Angie, Phil had a dog park behind his house too. Cody, Katie and I would wrestle and chase until we were too tired to move. There was plenty of shade in the park but I preferred to sun myself on the deck until that pesky Cody would launch another attack. Soon Katie would join in. Game on! Phil's house became our new home.

The best part of this new arrangement is that I would be reunited with Tim. While staying with Angie and later with Grandma, I kept a vigil by the front door each night, refusing food or water until Tim came through the door. Grandma would try and coax me into the kitchen late in the evening and encourage me to eat the food that had been sitting in my bowl since morning. Only when I was convinced that Tim's truck was not pulling into the driveway would I turn my attention to kibble.

Sometimes it was dark before Tim and Phil came through the door. Tim often looked tired and quickly retreated to the upstairs room with some fine smelling people food. After filling my bowl with kibble, he would turn on the box with moving pictures but pay little attention to it. Most of the time he lay prone on his back drifting in and out of sleep. There was pain all around us and it frustrated me because I did not understand it. Maybe he missed Grandma or our home. I know he missed Josh.

"I am for you," I repeated in bed each night as I rested my head on his leg.

But Tim just stared at the ceiling.

I once wondered what purpose there could possibly be for a dog with three legs.

Now it was clear. Something was terribly wrong with Tim, so I did what dogs have been doing since the first one of us wandered timidly into a human village. I kept him safe. I kept him warm.

"And if you want me to come with you
Then that's all right with me.
'Cause I know I'm goin' nowhere
And anywhere's a better place to be."

Harry Chapin, "A Better Place To Be"

CHAPTER 14: TIM THE TRAINER

Phil paid me what he could to be his tag-along. I was grateful but I still had a mortgage payment on an empty house in Topeka that was due at the first of each month. In good conscience, I could not ask Mom for any more than she had already given. It was clear that I would never work in my chosen field again and I began to think of what to do with the rest of my life in terms of a career. I signed on with an agency that doled out temporary work, thinking I might stumble into something I could love half as much as early education. One week I moved furniture, another week I processed forms in a medical office, and on a few summer nights I was a banquet server.

After a month of temp work, it finally dawned on me that most people are not defined by their work. Up to this point, I was a dad and I ran an early education center. The volunteer work that I had done was connected to kids. I had no hobbies, no unique talents and I only dabbled in sports. It occurred to me that I was actually quite dull. I was a dad in title only and had been permanently derailed from the only career I had ever known. Perhaps the healthiest people out there go to work to earn a living but come home to a life. Other than fatherhood, my life had always been at work.

The answer was sleeping at my feet each night. Dogs! I immediately went to my computer and completed an application with PetSmart. Several jobs were listed—night stocker, cashier, pet products manager, pet presentation manager, operations manager. It was all Greek to me.

But what's this? Pet trainer. Hmm. Teaching. Public speaking. Selling. I could do that.

Like any eager job applicant half my age, I researched the company and learned that PetSmart, Inc. is the largest pet retailer in this part of the world, with more than 1,200 stores in the United States, Canada and Puerto Rico at last count. Maybe it could fit one more cog in its corporate wheel.

I quickly uploaded my resume to the careers link at the PetSmart website and asked that it be forwarded to the store nearest Phil's house. Within a couple of days, I received a call from store manager Dave requesting an interview. My only retail experience came when I was sixteen working at a neighborhood pharmacy. I stocked shelves and made deliveries. One tends to raise a few eyebrows when you tell an interviewer that your first job in high school was running drugs in a 1976 Honda Civic roughly the size of a toaster.

Dave explained that if hired, I would be enrolled in a three week academy to prepare for the job. The first week would be spent in the store studying the intricacies of dog training inside a retail store. I would then be farmed out to a sister store in Independence, Missouri for two weeks to work with an area trainer named Ally. It all seemed perfectly acceptable. David said that pet trainers are paid an hourly wage and receive commissions from pet training classes sold. He remarked that pet trainers were in charge of their own destiny and that a comfortable living could be earned if I was committed to selling classes to customers.

"Sell" had always been a four letter word to me but a necessary evil in the world of non-profit work. Money was always scarce and there was great competition for available funds. Everyone had a worthy program but the pie could only be sliced so many ways. I was used to singing for my supper when I truly believed in the cause. Nowadays I wasn't sure what I believed in and I had not felt passionate about anything other than Dixie for a very long time. I began to second guess my decision to interview with the company. Too late. David called the next day with a job offer. I was hired by PetSmart as a pet trainer in November of 2006. The salary was considerably less money than I was making as the Early

Education Center director but at least I was working with the chance to be productive again.

I was pleased to see that PetSmart training classes were still based on positive reinforcement just as they were when Dixie participated. I discovered that training dogs and managing behavior in a preschool classroom or with Josh at home had striking similarities. Best of all, there was a wealth of credible science proving that reward based methods were the most effective way to train a dog.

The first week at PetSmart was spent in the Olathe, Kansas store reading the pet training accreditation manual and completing some simple exercises in the store. I was pretty much left alone to do this while encouraged to interact with customers. Once this would have been a no-brainer but I had spent the last three months avoiding people. It felt awkward approaching shoppers to ask if they needed assistance. At least I had something in common with these people. We all loved pets. Best of all, there was little chance of anyone recognizing me since the news feeds that inundated the Topeka air waves about my case still weren't newsworthy to the big city media machine.

Weeks two and three of my accreditation were spent with Ally in Independence. She appeared to be a competent trainer but had no idea what to do with the likes of me. Most of my first week was a repeat of what I had being doing at my home store in terms of customer service and reviewing the mind numbing accreditation manual. Observing her classes was helpful, as I watched her skillfully interact with the dogs and manage the class with almost military like efficiency. Although I respected her methods, I envisioned my own classes taking on a more lighthearted tone.

The final week with Ally was spent teaching her classes. I had grown weary of playing second fiddle to a woman nearly young enough to be my daughter and was ready to put my long-practiced public speaking skills to the test. Ally could not possibly have been aware of my resumé prior to PetSmart so was equally ignorant to my humiliation when she insisted on listening to some follow-up phone calls I was making on her behalf so she "could see how I did on the phone."

My first teaching assignment was to introduce the concept of "marking" behavior to a class of about six students and their dogs henceforth referred to as "teams."

Students are given two options in terms of marking their dog's correct behavior. First is the "clicker," a hand held device that makes a clicking sound when a button is pushed. The other was to mark behavior is with a word or phrase like "yes," "good boy/girl," "good dog," etc. The marker is then followed immediately with a reward that the dog defines as a pearl of great prize. It is most likely a tasty treat although could be a belly rub, tennis ball, or praise. Most dogs are motivated by some sort of food so it works as a primary means of reinforcement in pet training classes.

We know that dogs learn through associations. Open the pantry door where the kibble is stored and Dixie comes a-running. Holding out the leash produces a frenzy of spins (4 to be exact), then a reluctant sit followed the swaying of the head from side to side that reminds me of a sea lion just before the trainer tosses her a herring. On the other hand, opening a closet door in the bedroom likely produces little interest because Dixie doesn't associate it with anything she values.

Developing an association between the marker and the reward was known as "loading the clicker" in the PetSmart curriculum. I liked the way that sounded and so I introduced the concept as thoroughly as my three weeks of training allowed. As I completed what I thought was an effective explanation, I caught a student "loading" her clicker by shoving her pea-sized treats inside the tiny box that housed the clicking mechanism. I stood flabbergasted and turned to snarl at Ally, thinking I had just fell victim to some hazing ritual. Lo and behold, she had the same dumbfound expression on her face.

"Mr. Trainer, this thing don't click no more," the woman cried out. Much to Ally's amusement, I had been initiated into the world of pet training.

While teaching pet training classes was a relatively easy transition, selling pet training services to unsuspecting customers was another matter. By nature I am not a pushy person. Fund raising was the least favorite component of my job description back in my non-profit days. I could speak passionately about my cause to an audience of two or two hundred but got weak in the knees when it came to closing the deal. My goal was to sell four pet training classes during the two weeks I was in Independence. I sold three, no thanks to a winter blizzard that forced an early closing of the store on two occasions. It's tough to expound on the virtues of positive pet training when people are hunkering down for a pre-Christmas blizzard.

By early December, I was back at my home store in Olathe and teaching without a safety net. The "classroom" was little more than a series of canvas partitions strung together to form a 10 x 10 square in the middle of a busy retail store. The learning environment was compromised by inquisitive customers ("hey, what kind of dog is that?"), noise from dog adoptions that took place every Saturday, and the occasional rogue child that would wander into the classroom to pet the puppies. The real challenge was keeping the humans focused while one or two dogs barked incessantly throughout the hour long session. Eventually, I learned how to help students redirect this behavior, but it was a struggle in the early days.

I was paired with an experienced trainer named Angelique, an outwardly frail but strong minded trainer whom customers adored. She had quite a following at the store and I wondered why anyone would want to take one of my classes. We talked a lot during our shifts and I observed her classes from afar. There were some techniques I embraced and others I did not but the experience with her ultimately made me a better trainer.

PetSmart is a great company. Much about the corporate culture was appealing. The notion of "every pet, every customer, every time" resonated with me. Perhaps this philosophy elevates PetSmart above competitors that sacrifice customer service to shave pennies off the price of merchandise. I also love the charitable side of the company that provides resources to help homeless pets and signed on to have a sliver of my paycheck set aside for PetSmart Charities.

"Saw my picture in the paper
Read the news around my face
And now some people don't want to treat me the same
When the walls come tumblin' down . . ."

John Mellencamp/George Michael Green, *"Crumblin' Walls"*

CHAPTER 15: FROM BAD TO WORSE

The Shawnee County Court system maintained a website that allowed me access to the DA's notes regarding my case. Almost daily I logged on with my case number to see if any decisions had been made about formally filing charges against me. The holiday season passed and I began to think my Christmas gift in 2006 was a dismissal of the case. In January of 2007, the District Attorney announced that I had been charged with *felony* indecent liberties with a child. The news quickly reached the electronic and print media and that hideous mug shot was again flashed all over Topeka. I was so thankful to be in Kansas City and wished my family and friends could join me.

The anxiety monster again raised its ugly head and I started back up with my medication. There were pills to quiet the runaway freight in my mind; pills that seemed to induce a coma an hour before bedtime; and pills to mute those demons telling me to take the easy way out. I've always hated taking medication for anything and was determined to maintain the recommended dosage no matter how bleak things became. I wasn't going down as a junkie. That much was certain.

PetSmart knew nothing of my case and I had planned to keep it that way until charges were officially filed. That time had come and the company was no longer on a need-to-know basis. I had been teaching for just over three months and was on good terms with new manager Vince as well as Jennifer, his brash German born second in command.

At the close of a shift one evening in March, I pulled Vince aside and told him everything. He was sympathetic, supportive, and assured me that he had no concerns about my "character." In fact, I had met his teenage daughter on several occasions and had developed a friendship with her. Vince said he would have no trouble with me continuing that friendship despite my confession. I took that as an affirmation and cherished it amidst the various on-line assaults to my character. There was one caveat. As a matter of protocol, Vince would have to inform the district manager.

About a week later, Vince asked to see me in his office where Jennifer and Angelique were waiting. Their serious expressions set an ominous tone and I knew that no good was to come from this meeting. Vince handed me a letter written by a faceless name from Human Resources. I was to be placed on an unpaid leave of absence until the trial and then reinstated "upon the successful resolution of your legal issues." Translation—I would be welcomed back if my new address wasn't Leavenworth. I could retain my benefits if I chose to pay for them. There would be no severance pay. Vince apologized and then escorted me from the premises. The trial date had not been set. I had no idea when or if I would ever return to work for PetSmart.

I returned to my little bedroom at Phil's house and told him of the news. He was enraged. I was planning to head back to Topeka with my tail between my legs but Phil insisted that I stay and help him with insurance claims once again. I was thankful for the opportunity, as I had no desire to be sequestered in Topeka until the trial. At least in Kansas City I could move about town without looking over my shoulder. Phil was, as always, the personification of friendship. Given this latest setback, I'm sure it took all he had to keep me emotionally afloat.

Phil had some odd jobs that needed done as well. In nine short months, I had gone from the director of a large early education center to picking up after Phil's dogs and mowing lawns. The low point came when one guy tossed a bucket on the driveway and told me to use it as a latrine because he didn't want me tracking dirt into the house. Unemployment had proved almost as humbling as parenting or training a dog.

Most of my time in the spring of 2007 was spent carrying Phil's equipment as we hopped roofs looking for hail and wind damage. Ascending and descending the steep pitch of a two story home with a wood shingle roof was about as much fun as a spinal tap and equally treacherous. It astounded me that Phil was as sure footed as a cliff dwelling mountain goat at the ripe old age of forty six and I wondered how much longer he would physically be able to do this kind of work. We were both exhausted at day's end and I quickly retired to my 12x14 haven on the second floor of his home where Dixie would greet me with spins, leaps, and kisses on the chin. I tended to get more of those late in the day when the razor stubble had settled in. It must feel good on a smooth pink tongue so I have always slept better knowing the experience was mutually gratifying.

By early spring of 2007, I had grown tired of living like a gypsy in between guest bedrooms. I therefore made the decision to rent out my Topeka house, get a permanent job and find an apartment in Kansas City. Renting the house was much easier than I expected, as applicants clamored to plunk down a security deposit and move in. I chose a law student and his wife who was a social worker. The income from the rent checks paid the mortgage which freed up money for the apartment.

Rental housing was abundant in Kansas City. I eventually chose an apartment complex in the city of Overland Park in Johnson County, Kansas. "OP" was once thought of as a suburb of Kansas City but is now one of the five most populated cities in the state. Johnson County's median income is well above state and national averages. Homes here are generally spacious and come in three shades of brown. Lawns are manicured. There are exactly 2.5 children and a Golden Retriever behind every privacy fence. Suburbia.

Though I had never lived in Overland Park, I was familiar with the apartment complex that became my new home. Phil had rented a unit back in his swinging single days. Before Josh was born, Yvonne and I would occasionally spend a weekend with him. The place was spacious as apartments go but considerably smaller than my Topeka house. I wondered how Dixie would adjust. Then it occurred to me that we had been living out of Hotel Phil for the past few months. No doubt the new apartment would seem downright roomy to her. Best of all, it was ours.

"Though you've grown away
No matter how you'll change, I'll know you
And when you tire of life alone,
There will always be one sure way back home . . ."

Kenny Loggins, "Cody's Song"

CHAPTER 16: LOST IN THE DESERT

In May I drove to Arizona to spend some time with Josh. He was struggling with his grades just as he had done in Topeka after his fifth grade year. By now he was failing nearly every subject. Josh's IQ had once tested out at 105 and there were no detectable learning disabilities. His ADHD was always an obstacle but I never allowed him to use it as an excuse for not completing his work. For whatever reason, he no longer took his medication and was in an academic nosedive. I could monitor his progress thanks to an Internet portal. Comments from his teachers were essentially the same. Nice kid, smart enough, just doesn't do his work. I had hoped that my visit would be a shot in the arm.

Prescott, AZ is a comfortable two day drive which meant an overnight at a Motel 6. Say what you will about Motel 6 but the rooms are clean and comfortable just like Mr. Bodette deadpans in his commercials. Best of all, they allow dogs of all sizes at no extra charge. Dixie has stayed in Motel 6 lodges in Kansas, Colorado, Utah, Arizona, Nebraska, Wyoming, Montana, Idaho, and Washington. I always ask for the queen size bed so that she can sleep the Eskimo way but inevitably she camps in two or three places throughout the night just as she does at home. I had traded off my beloved Toyota truck for a sedan and a lower car payment. Unemployment makes you do things like that. At least there was more room for Dixie inside.

When taking the northern route via I-70, we always make it a point to stop somewhere in the Rockies for a quick hike to break the monotony of glaring through a bug stained windshield for hours at a time. Dixie finds nothing more refreshing than a dip in a frigid mountain stream. Labs typically take to water like an eagle to flight but the loss of one webbed paw creates some buoyancy issues. In the water, Dixie is the Titanic right after it collides with the iceberg.

In fact, I once took her to a public pool that was sponsoring a "doggie dip." Many community pools sponsor these events on the last day before the water is drained for the season. Before I had a chance to change into my suit, Dixie belly busted into the deep end before discovering there were no visible means of escaping her watery prison. The teenage lifeguards had all but checked out for the season so it became necessary for me to jump in fully clothed and rescue my humiliated hound before she sunk into Davy Jones' locker. Lesson learned. Dixie now wades in, paddles about, and then quickly returns to shore. Her excursions into the icy Colorado waters are brief but nonetheless refreshing.

We also take the southern route to Arizona compliments of historic Route 66. A favorite stop is Gallup, New Mexico where there is a trail on the west end of town that weaves through the desert and takes about an hour to hike. Dixie is in her element when hiking, leaping effortlessly from the trail, into the woods and across large rocks as though she was indigenous to the land. Seldom does she hint of fatigue or a need to pull over and rest. Even on three legs, her stamina is equal to that of a plow horse and I marvel as she follows a scent without ever losing sight of me.

We arrived in Prescott exactly 24 hours after we left Overland Park. Dixie remained at the Prescott Motel 6 and I picked up Josh at his home in the unimpressive little community of Chino Valley, Arizona. The town could have easily been called "Desloate Valley," as there was little growth beyond weeds and sagebrush. A strong westerly wind blew unabated, leaving the ground rocky and unforgiving. Josh was living in drafty single wide mobile home.

My little boy was becoming a young man. I was not accustomed to such dramatic changes in growth. It's hard to notice those things when you see your child every day. Josh was proud of some facial fuzz that he proclaimed could only be fully appreciated when the sun was out. In Arizona, the sun can be seen on the average of 300 days a year so I would have many opportunities to gaze upon my son's mustache which looked more like a chocolate milk stain above his lip.

His hair was several different lengths, having been victimized by his mother's amateur attempts at sheep shearing. I had Josh's hair trimmed regularly by a professional barber named Duane. Old Duane would be turning cartwheels in his grave if he could see this hatchet job. Hygiene had taken a holiday and his teeth looked like something out of "Deliverance." I later noticed that Josh never brought a toothbrush when he traveled to Kansas for a visit.

I was curious to ask Josh what his mother had said about the accusation. Just days after my arrest, detective Linquist had called Yvonne in Arizona and told her everything. I received a seething e-mail from her (one of many sent over the years) that had me all but drawn and quartered over not disclosing the entire story. Up to that point, I had only revealed that I quit my job at Christ The King Early Education Center but chose to withhold information about the arrest and ongoing criminal case. Yvonne and I had been on shaky ground for years. We were always at odds about what was best for Josh, especially in matters of child custody, visitation, child support, etc. I was concerned that she would use the sordid details of the past few months to forever taint my relationship with Josh. Sure enough, my worst suspicions were realized when I asked Josh what he knew of my situation.

"Mom said you raped some kid."

My heart was in free-fall. I paused before putting together a description of the events without chastising his mother. All the while I was silently cursing her name and quite likely her parentage. How dare she say such a thing! What could Josh be thinking? Josh looked out the car window and nodded occasionally as I explained. I told him how much I needed him to believe in me and that his support would be a source of strength as I navigated through the troubled waters ahead. He wasn't buying it. I could tell. The poison has already run its course.

The time we spent hiking, eating out, and catching a movie or two was strained and awkward. Josh gave little more than broken sentences when asked a question and seemed to grow weary of my inquiries that were of the "tell me what's going on in your life" variety. It was invasive but Josh reacted as though it were an inquisition.

Prescott and the surrounding area boast hiking trails that provide a panoramic view of the Bradshaw Mountain range and even the San Francisco Peaks near Flagstaff. Josh's favorite hiking venue is called Granite Dells. He confessed that his mother had taken him there but stayed in the car while he hiked. While we were married, Yvonne was to aerobic exercise what a cat would be to a bath so this came as no surprise. Josh was a bushwhacker, preferring to ditch the trail in favor of scaling majestic rocks brilliantly carved by water and wind over millions of years. The formations were stunning and provided a natural fortress for a crystal blue lake.

As usual, Dixie's antics unknowingly (or maybe she did know) gave us something to talk about as the conversation on the trail began to drag. I was skeptical as to whether she could navigate the rock faces and treacherous descents. But Dixie proved again to be no ordinary tripod. Rather, she was more like some crazed mountain goat on meth, climbing the rocks with impressive displays of strength and agility. The Dells were her playground. Josh and I could only sit back, marvel, and try to find the words that adequately described the show we were privileged to view. We were in awe as Dixie scaled a nearly impossible incline, then wedged through the crevice between two boulders only to take on another.

"We better stop, Dad." Josh said. "She'll never make that one." He was clearly worried about her.

Suddenly we gazed upward at Dixie standing at the precipice and shaking her head as if to say, *"I'm growing old up here—are you two coming or not?"*

Then we would laugh. Yes, we laughed. And for that moment, albeit a brief one, all was forgotten and we were father and son again.

On our third and final day together, we lunched at a little burger place just a short walk from his home. The food was fantastic but we were running out of things to say. For some reason, Josh ordered hot tea—not exactly the drink of choice with a cheeseburger. I spent most of the meal watching him experiment with different blends. We then returned to the house. Josh suddenly became very uncomfortable as I followed him inside. His mother was at work. I asked if everything was alright.

"Mom doesn't want you in our house."

I was stunned but managed to hold it together, saying that I understood when in fact my blood was boiling inside. As I reached the door, I went to hug my son goodbye. His forced embrace left me chilled to the bone for it was without feeling. Tears streaked my face as I got into the car only to look upon Dixie lying solemnly in the back seat. It was time to go home.

It would be months before I would see Josh again. Most of my calls went unreturned but I faithfully left messages twice a week, sent cards, and wrote letters. Yes, letters. "Snail mail" as they say nowadays. This ancient form of correspondence is a lost art in a world now saturated with Tweets, Facebook, and that relic known as e-mail. I thought maybe he would take notice if I actually took the time to write something, stuff it into in an envelope and paste a stamp on it. In truth, I had no idea as to whether he was even receiving his mail.

INSIGHTS: LONELY BUT NOT ALONE

While I am for Tim, it has become apparent to me that Tim is for Josh. Part of me is for Josh as well. Tim misses Josh so much that it hurts him inside. I feel his pain so I lay close by when he feels most alone. In that way we have each other for company. Some days even that doesn't seem enough.

Long car rides meant we got to see Josh. These were the happiest of times. His body was changing. He was taller and his voice sounded more like an adult human. He seemed happy to see us and couldn't wait go hiking. Tim would let Josh pick the trail and his favorite was near a lake surrounded by giant rocks. I watched Josh climb them and I quickly followed. Before I knew it, I had passed Tim and Josh and then waited impatiently as they inched their way to the top. This was more fun than chasing those stupid rabbits and a lot safer because there were no cars in sight.

Tim was very quiet on the journey home. Saying goodbye to Josh made him very sad. Sometimes he would reach into the backseat and scratch my ears while he drove. His hands were lifeless and the sparkle in his eyes had faded. Tim was returning to the place where he felt most alone. Clearly my vacation was over too.

Dogs get lonely too. I must confess that I am afraid of being alone. It terrified me when I first came to live with Tim. I wasn't sure he would ever come back. It felt a little like being a tie down dog except there was no chain around my neck. The difference was that he always came home and we shared a moment when I was the center of his world. Those moments made it worth the wait.

Some days I stayed in a big room at the pet store while Tim worked. I caught glimpses of him moving about but he did not come for me until it was time to go home. This I did not understand. There were other dogs for company and sometimes I played with them but it just wasn't the same. I am not for them. I am for Tim. Why were we apart? Seeing him made me so anxious to be with him that I barked and jumped at the window while the other dogs chased a silly ball around the room.

I am afraid of other things too. The rumble that comes from the sky makes my chest ache. Leaning against Tim calms me. The one place that smells most like Tim is his bed so I lay curled up there when the rumbles come and he is away.

For the most part, cars don't frighten as they once did. I still get jumpy when the giant ones pass too close. Humans like to ride bikes that growl and I am often startled as they roar by. People seem to like things that make noise. Dogs prefer the quiet. I'm glad I'm a dog.

Oh yes, those balloons that carry people around scare the kibble right out of me. Literally. People shoot fire into them and it makes the most awful sound. I bark at them when they pass overhead but they just ignore me and spit more fire.

Humans like to put statues of people or things in their yard throughout the year. Sometimes there is a machine underneath that makes wind. To a dog, it makes the thing look very much alive. One winter day, I growled at one to stay back. As we passed by, an old woman told her man that I was trying to eat Jesus. I have no idea what that meant but it caused Tim to pull my leash tight so that we could walk faster. We never walked past that house again.

Nothing terrifies a dog more than being separated from the people that care for us. I know dogs that spend the majority of their moments this way. Why do people get dogs and then leave them alone? We cry out for you and suddenly we are wearing collars that shock us or spray a stinging mist in our nose. Those collars are terrifying and confuse us. When that doesn't work, you send us to another home or back to live with other dogs. Worse yet, you turn us into tie-down dogs. You brought us into your home. We want to be with you. Don't you want to be with us?

"How much does it cost?
I'll buy it
The time is all we've lost
I'll try it . . ."

Jonathan Edwards, "Sunshine"

CHAPTER 17: SOUL FOR SALE

PetSmart's decision to place me on indefinite leave forced my return to the job (meat) market. Despite a recessive economy, I had three job offers within weeks after returning home from Arizona.

The first was from a retail competitor. I was leery, as they actually sold puppies. PetSmart was all about adopting dogs and cats rather than classifying them as them inventory.

As I researched the company, I learned that their puppies came from large scale breeding operations known as "puppy mills." Missouri is home to an estimated 3,000 puppy mills whose practices have come under much needed scrutiny in the past few years. More than 80 percent of the puppies sold to pet stores come from puppy mills where care of the animals takes a back seat to profit. Some operations hoard hundreds of animals on their property. The breeding dogs seldom leave the confines of their kennels and exist only to multiply. Genetic screenings for health problems common to some breeds are bypassed. Puppies travel half-way across the country and arrive at these stores traumatized and under socialized. Impulse driven consumers then pay ridiculously marked up prices for puppies that are sick, genetically flawed, and emotionally damaged.

Working for a company that knowingly subsidized the puppy mill industry was just wrong. As a strong advocate of pet adoption, I would be no less the hypocrite for signing on with them.

That left just two legitimate contenders. The first was a corporate position with a local utility company. My job would be to sit in a cubicle and advise callers where they could safely dig to avoid an unpleasant encounter with underground power lines. The pay was a step up from PetSmart but the job had all the appeal of lukewarm beer.

The third option was a sales job for a local General Motors dealership. The lot featured Buicks for the senior set, Pontiacs for the young as well as those stuck in a mid-life tar pit, and GMC trucks for people who felt they needed such a thing in the middle of flat, paved, middle class suburbia.

Although currently driving a Mercury sedan, I was a Toyota and Honda man at heart and wrestled with selling a product I would never personally own. Still, this was not quite the moral dilemma I faced with selling sick puppies to an unsuspecting public. I concluded that I would eventually be fired by the utility company for either snoozing in my cubicle or instructing some poor soul to dig directly into a power line and turning him into a human French fry.

In June of 2007, I become a car salesman.

"Down time" is a term used to describe one's less productive hours. In the car business, down time is the only time. You are paid an hourly wage but can only survive on the commission from sales. Ed, Karen and Bob were the three experienced sales people. They had repeat customers. That left another rookie salesman and me to canvas the new car lot in search of an unsuspecting customer and pounce like a leopard from the treetops. We were the predators of the car sales jungle. Perhaps the reputation of car sales people is earned, for we make our living off the impulses of the buyer. The real money can be made selling pre-owned cars where the mark ups are at times obscene. Surprisingly, the mark up on a new car is modest and so is the commission. This was not going to be easy.

For hours I would sit mindlessly at a table overlooking the new car lot. There were sales associates assigned to pre-owned cars and that was forbidden ground unless the customer specifically asked us to show them a vehicle from that lot. There were technical manuals to be studied containing all the features of the various vehicles sold. They were about as interesting to me as watching paint dry and I quickly learned that I lacked the passion for cars that the other sales associates seemed to possess. While they could chat about car specs for hour after dreary hour, I made small talk and retreated to my little table overlooking the new car lot.

Desperate to pass the empty hours, I began to keep a journal. I needed a mode of expression for the private hell I was living each day and writing had been my chosen forum since I was young. I wasn't particularly good at car sales. While I could effectively engage the customer, I lacked the fortitude to close the sale when it required me to be the least bit confrontational.

While I scribbled on my legal pad, the other sales people planned bull sessions at the bar, dinner with their families and tee times at the public golf course. I didn't drink, barely ate, and despised golf. The gap between us widened to the point where we did little more than exchange pleasantries. My sales numbers were modest at best.

"Don't you do anything around here?" quipped an elderly customer as he walked past my writer's guild in a corner of the showroom floor.

He was kidding, of course, but the comment ate away at me like a summer parasite for several days. He was right. My work in the non-profit world mattered. As a car sales person, I was as useful as a rubber crutch.

One day, sales manager Ryan produced some monthly car payment options that were $100 over what my customer was willing to pay. I cringed when Ryan handed me his figures.

"Don't be afraid, just show him the numbers." Ryan said with a scowl.

Disgusted, I snatched the paper from his hand and returned to the customer. He glanced at the offer from the dealership and walked out of the showroom mumbling something under his breath and I nearly followed suit. This was not going to be a career path for me.

Ryan was right and the truth cut me like a dagger. I was afraid and the comment made me stop and take stock of my life and where this accusation had taken me. Although I had Dixie, friends, and family in my corner, there were days where it just didn't seem to matter. After a midnight walk, I sat down at the computer with Dixie sleeping at my feet and wrote the following:

> *"I will never be me again; I am afraid for my own life; my son is a stranger to me; I am uninspired; I am disconnected; I am a refugee; there is no point to me being here; I sell cars; someone else lives in my house; I will grow old alone; I keep my distance; I play it safe; I will never be in a position to be hurt by anyone again; I am numb; the nights are short; The days are uneventful; I listen to sad songs; I no longer play; I am wasting away; I am ashamed of my name."*

I wrote about the yearning I had for my son and what I missed most about being his dad in the early years:

> *Dear Josh:*
>
> *I miss: Your sweet voice; a perfectly round face that launched a thousand smiles; your button nose; how time stood still while I watched you sleep; 4 a.m., a blue recliner, a bottle," binky," and "House at Pooh Corner;" the 4 "B's"—bath, Barney®, book, and bed; singing 'I Don't Want to Walk Without You' at 10:35 p.m.; January 13, 1994 and a thousand times after that; 'Aristocats' and 'Go Dog, Go' over and over and over and over . . . ; reading my essay, 'Baby's First Christmas,' at church in 1995; Saturday morning pony rides and lunch at McDonald's®; tumbling into my bed just before sunrise mumbling 'snuggle Daddy;' floor time; Gage Park and feeding the ducks; Grandpa; Sunday dinner at Grandma's; haircuts with Duane; the zoo.*

Then I made out my will. This was my literary pity party. For a time, it kept the demons at bay.

"Hanzie" was my first dog

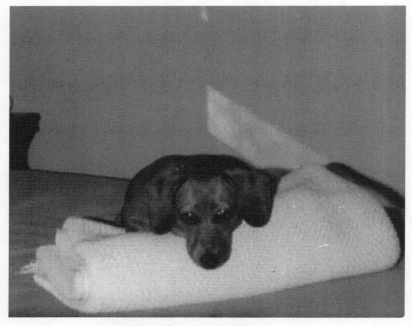

Then came Hilde

Princess making sure the new Daddy gets it right.

This photo was taken by shelter staff just after Dixie arrived.

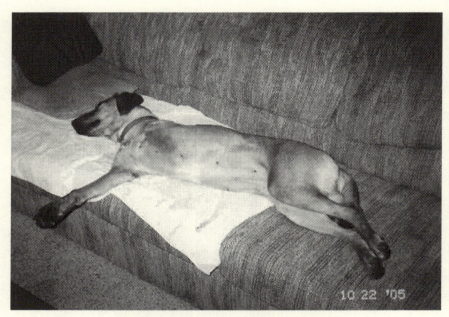

October 22, 2005. Dixie's first day home.
Notice the bruising around her scar.

Who has the bigger smile, Josh or Dixie?

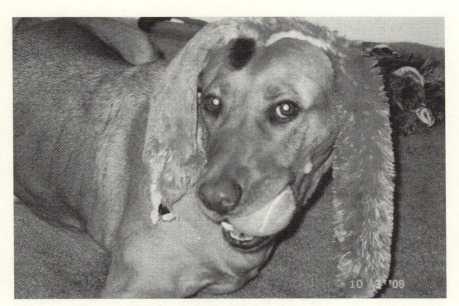

Look, I'm a Bloodhound!

One of my favorites. Can you see the treat on her front paw?

Dixie and good friends Lydia, Bella, Ary, and Layne

Dixie takes the morning watch over Josh

Hiking at Granite Dells, Prescott, AZ

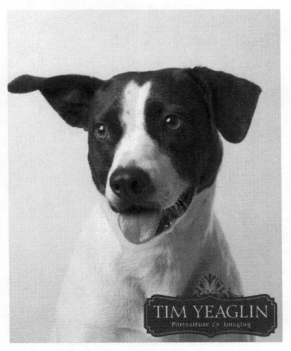

Oreo

It's the most wonderful time of the year!

Arnold Dog Park just outside of St. Louis

"Dogtoberfest" agility exhibition

Our first agility title!

"Pooches on the Parkway" exhibition

A weaving machine (ignore the hairy drumsticks running alongside)

Strike the pose

Winter fun at Stoll Park

Dixie and Oreo

Tumor removal, compliments of Dr. Barnes

Dixie and Oreo love the mountains too

Rest stop on the trail in Estes Park, CO

Crashing after a Rocky Mountain high

Enjoying a summer dip in Boulder, CO

Tim really captured the essence of my dog with this one

Agility pals Oliver (left) and Cora

Carol Stubbs, the best friend a dog ever had

Dr. Darrell Carder saved Dixie's life in 2005

"My shadow's the only one that walks beside me
My shallow heart's the only thing that's beating
Sometimes I wish someone out there will find me
'Til then I walk alone . . ."

Green Day, "Boulevard of Broken Dreams"

CHAPTER 18: AFRAID

When referencing customers with no cash, a sales colleague said "they don't have enough money to buy steam off a cheeseburger." Such was the state of my finances within a month after taking the job. My monthly net income was less than $1,200 which was absorbed by rent, child support, Josh's health insurance and my car payment, say nothing about utilities, food, Josh's college fund, and Dixie.

I had invested some money inherited from Dad's estate. Legal fees were eating away at that nest egg and I was certain it would all but be devoured by the time my trial came around. Bankruptcy was looming and that reality added even more stress to my days.

It all hit critical mass one day at the dealership when I logged into the district court website one Monday in July and discovered that the prosecution had subpoenas out to my former employers that required them to turn over my personnel records. My employment record was solid and without incident. Still, the thought of people having access to all facets of my private and professional life was unnerving at best.

The prosecution had also asked for a deadline extension for turning over their evidence to my legal team. I placed a frantic call to legal assistant and new confidant Jane Laptad. She believed the prosecution needed more time to review personnel records that they should have requested months ago. Or was it something else? Jane didn't think so and temporarily put my mind at ease. Jane then asked if I could meet her at the Early Education Center later in the week to photograph the meeting room where the alleged incident took place. The idea of setting foot in that building again sent chills down my spine. But I agreed to meet her.

I pulled into the parking lot as I had done hundreds of times while I was the director of the center and waited for Jane. I was several minutes early so there was nothing to do but scan my favorite radio stations for a soothing song. As the time for our rendezvous approached, my airway began to constrict. In a strangled voice, I called Jane and told her I just couldn't go through with it. I scurried away like a frightened child and drove back to Overland Park. If I had a tail, it would have been tucked between my legs. It wasn't until I took Dixie on an evening walk that my heart rate returned to normal.

Jane understood. She was special that way. At times she was quirky, eccentric, and irreverent. Around the office she cursed like a sailor. On this day she was my empathetic friend who did not sit in judgment of my weakened emotional state. Jane was truly an enigma and a character for the ages.

Random doom and gloom scenarios began flooding my conscious thoughts. My physician increased the dosage of Lorazepam.

"If I ever get through this," I told Phil over lunch one day, "I'm going to write a book."

I found two natural havens from the onslaught of panic and anxiety that were my nemesis during the summer of 2007. The first was a counselor recommended to me by the pastor of the church I occasionally attended. Coincidentally, that person was the pastor's husband. Tom agreed to see me weekly on Sunday evenings *pro bono*. I will never forget his compassionate and insightful guidance.

The second, of course, was Dixie. Together we discovered local hiking trails, off leash parks, and dog-friendly suburban strolls. We had not trained in some time so I began incorporating exercises in our walks. There was an ample yard with lush green grass surrounding the tennis courts and we practiced commands there as well. In time, I could place her in a "stay" or "wait," move fifty yards, and circle her several times while she remained in place. We practiced off leash "heel" on the tennis court using the white boundary lines to maintain precision. For Dixie, the basics came easy. Pleasing me was all that seemed to matter and she quickly returned to form. Though our bond was airtight, we did have our moments.

One night, we took our customary 10 p.m. off leash constitutional across the complex to an empty field so that Dixie could chase the vermin across the dormant summer grass. Typically, I called her back and she eventually meandered to my side with her tongue flapping out the side of her mouth. For some reason, she paused as I called to her and then darted off into the darkness toward the apartment building closest to the field. Though sufficiently annoyed by this apparent act of defiance, I maintained a cheerful tone as I called her name through the musty night air. Several minutes passed and there was no Dixie. I began to pace the field as my call backs became more frantic. I then circled the building where I last spied my mischievous mutt and returned to the field in case she had doubled back. She was nowhere in sight.

I swear there are times I can read her thoughts as easily as the nonsensical rhymes of a Dr. Seuss book. It's like we're connected by some kind of cosmic heartstring. Something told me to return to my tiny apartment amongst this labyrinth of buildings just to see if Dixie made it home. I came around the corner of my building and there was my dog with a smug *"where the hell have you been?"* look on her face. I said nothing and barely offered her a parting glance as I got ready for bed. Dixie abandoned her favorite night time roost at the foot of my bed and opted for the couch. We had experienced our first marital spat.

Jane gently insisted that we reschedule the photo session at the Early Education Center. Much like a root canal, there was no escaping it this time. I somehow managed to harness my cowardly energy and escorted her into the meeting room where Alice alleged the abuse took place nearly a year ago. Jane helped me arrange the room as I remembered it that day.

The child claimed we sat down and played a "game." In reality, the room had not been set up for the seminar that evening by the custodial staff.

Eventually, I had delegated that task to a teacher because I had a million things to get done in preparation for the gathering.

"I can't believe my future as a free man rides on the setup of a room," I told Jane as she snapped pictures with her digital camera.

Without a witness who could say they saw me in my office or in that room with the child for a mere 30 seconds, what defense did I have? Once my personnel records arrived in the DA's office, they would soon find that their case rested on the testimony of a delusional little girl. Surely that was not enough evidence to convict me.

I met Mom for dinner later that evening. She insisted on coming to the trial and we argued the wisdom on that decision. This was going to get ugly and I worried about her ability to endure the stress. No parent should have to sit quietly while her child is portrayed as some kind of deviant. Her strength throughout this ordeal had been nothing short of extraordinary. Only she knew the hell I had put her through and perhaps that was the greatest casualty of all.

A pre-trial hearing was scheduled for August 17. Don said it was nothing more than a formality but it quickly turned into a nightmare. Citing an unpublished case from the seventies, a sharp young prosecutor moved to make the offense an "off grid felony." If convicted, I faced 25 years to life in prison. We were given the option of waving the preliminary hearing and going straight to trial.

It all seemed so ridiculously unfair. Michael Vick served considerably less time for funding and participating in the mindless brutality known as dog fighting where unworthy dogs are disposed of by electrocution and drowning. Some singer named R. Kelly slept with a 15-year-old and got probation, thus allowing him to rake in millions in record sales. In other news, a local CEO of a large utility saddled the poor with higher utility bills by embezzling millions from shareholders.

"Where's the justice in any of this?" I vented to Jane over the phone. "I will take my innocent plea to the grave. I didn't touch this child!"

This burden was not mine alone to bear. Family and friends shared in it and it troubled me deeply. Because Don wanted to go through with the preliminary hearing, the trial tentatively set for September would be pushed back, thus dragging this sordid mess out even longer.

During the pre-trial hearing, the prosecution requested that certain comments from the interrogation be deleted. I asked Jane for her opinion and she sided with Don.

"Hell, no!" she said. "If they want to admit the interrogation as evidence, that means all of it and not just selected portions. Don and I believe it stands up well as is."

I was in complete agreement. I was tired of conceding and compromising. What had it produced so far?

My chest hurt after meeting with Don and Jane. My eyes were puffy and sore from fading in and out of sleep. My head was pounding, my heart raced, and my mouth was dry. I could not concentrate and was preoccupied with my fate. This was no way to live.

"When darkness comes
And pain is all around
Like a bridge over troubled water
I will lay me down..."

Paul Simon/Art Garfunkel, "Bridge Over Troubled Water"

CHAPTER 19: GROUND ZERO

And with that experience recorded in my journal for posterity, I had reached "ground zero." In a state of utter despair, I left my apartment with Dixie on leash. I was not coming back.

A short distance from my apartment was a corporate complex and a walking path encircling a pond. It was Dixie's favorite constitutional. Once we reached the path, I would remove the leash and let her frolic about as I watched the ducks and geese float effortlessly on the waterfront from the rail overlooking the pond. Generally, my so-called bird dog had no interest in them, as the adjacent field abounded with rabbits and squirrels that required her attention. Sometimes she would jump into the pond to cool off and send the water fowl scurrying for cover. It usually brought a smile to my face but not on this night.

I used my cell phone to call Mom one last time. The conversation began with "I'm having a real bad night." She replied with those motherly words of wisdom that often gave me the strength to carry on another day. Tonight, they rang strangely shallow. I ended the conversation with "I love you." It was a sentiment shared more frequently over the past several months.

I then was alone with Dixie, my steadfast companion for the past two years. She wasn't going to talk me out of this. I'm a lousy swimmer and a railing was the only thing that separated me from a watery demise. My youth baseball coaches instructed us never to swim on a game day. Almost every day was a game day so I spent little time in the water. I could swim well enough to remain afloat for a few hundred yards but would eventually sink like a stone.

The will was in place. Mortgage insurance would pay off my house. My estate would require minimal effort to close. Maybe I could endure a few more months of this but I was no longer willing to stand by and watch my mother worry herself into the grave nor could I live with what this was doing to my friends.

I looked to Dixie who had all but lost interest in the critters afoot and sat solemnly at my side. I looked down at my dog for the last time.

"With me to the end. You deserve so much better than the life I had to offer. Angie will see that you get a better home."

And with that I grasped the rail and . . . .

. . . turned to see my stupid dog sprinting toward the water in hot pursuit of a wayward goose she had ignored for the past year. The goose honked a warning to its fellow fowl and the stillness of a summer night was interrupted by a drum roll of wings and a shower of feathers that settled harmlessly on the water's surface. I stepped back from the railing and shouted a curse at Dixie as if somehow that would be an incentive for her to return to my side.

"Goddammit get back here!" I screamed. "Can't you see I'm trying to kill myself?"

Lost in the absurdity of the moment, I did what most people would do when a suicide attempt is interrupted by a fowl fetching Labrador. I laughed. Then I fell to the sidewalk in a fetal position and I cried like a brokenhearted child. I guess they call that catharsis. I would live to laugh another day. But this moment was as desperate as any I can recall to this day. A goose-chasing tripod named Dixie had just saved my life.

Jane Laptad and I would spend a great deal of time together building my case through the remainder of August and into September. Both she and

Don were determined to go to trial. Their commitment towards proving my innocence gave me an injection of much-needed hope as the time for the preliminary hearing grew near. Once Jane and I reconstructed the alleged crime scene at Christ The King, the events of that fateful day were pieced together like a jigsaw puzzle.

Thanks to Jane's research, we learned that both the police and Child Protective Services violated their own procedures in the investigation. For example, the law entitled us to a copy of the video interview with the child conducted by a young social worker. At no point did she establish that Alice could distinguish a lie from the truth. Rather, her questions led the child to believe that something traumatic actually took place thus giving credibility to her fabrication. The video tape of my interrogation evoked laughter from the entire legal staff as detective Lindquist tried desperately to strong arm a confession from me. No wonder the DA wanted parts of it struck from the proceedings.

Jane and I went to dinner after watching the interrogation on a TV in her office. She confessed that she did not believe my story when we first met. In fact, my case triggered some trauma from her own childhood, as she was a victim of sexual abuse herself. She initially wanted nothing to do with me and cringed at the firm's decision to take my case. Legal assistants do much of the legwork and research to prepare for a trial lawyer's appearance on center stage. Jane knew we would be spending time together and initially was none too thrilled at this prospect.

Post-traumatic stress would take its toll on my new friend as preparations for this trial became more intense. Every minute of that fateful day was being scrutinized and documented. Memories that had haunted Jane all these years began to surface. We talked for hours about her experiences over lunch one day and in the office long after everyone had left. The victim from all those years ago and the recently accused had found common spiritual ground. Jane believed we would win.

Slowly, I began to believe too.

Jane had an odd question during a September meeting.

"What shoes were you wearing that day? Jane inquired with a hint of urgency in her voice.

I was perplexed by the question and paused to think for a moment. How hard could this be? I'm a dude. I only owned four pair. There were the beloved hiking boots that accompanied me on local walking trails with Dixie, my running shoes for the 10 miles Dixie and I logged each week in the wee hours of the morning, and the everyday casuals I wore to work.

THE DRESS SHOES! I wore the leather slip on shoes that day.

A disclosure such as this normally doesn't warrant such enthusiasm but on this day it was appropriate. The little girl stated in her video that she untied my shoe laces as a part of some perverted ritual that took place in meeting room "C." It's no wonder that so many believed this child. Her account of the afternoon's events was too bizarre not to be taken as truth. Meeting room "C" was being set up because of an educational in-service I had scheduled for the staff that evening. As a result, I had abandoned jeans and casual shoes for a more professional look that included the leather slip on shoes. There were no shoe strings to untie. Jan had discovered our ace in the hole. It was beginning to sound like OJ and the glove defense.

The preliminary hearing was set for mid-August of 2007. Unlike the pre-trial fiasco, it was little more than a formality. The charge was read and I entered an adamant "not guilty" plea in the court of the Honorable Nancy Parrish. A trial was set for the last week in September. There was nothing to do now but prepare. And wait.

Don called me into his office a week after the preliminary hearing. The DA's Office had offered a plea bargain. The sentence would be significantly reduced if I agreed to plead guilty and serve no more than 18 months in jail. While this was a far cry from the 25 to life cloud hanging over my head, I would still be going to jail for a crime I did not commit.

"Hell, no!" I replied to Don. "Tell 'em we'll see their happy asses in court."

And with that bit of uncharacteristic belligerence, we were off to trial.

In athletics there is an expression about "putting on your game face" before an important competition. I had been wearing mine for the six weeks leading up to the trial. There was a lot at stake here. For starters, my freedom. Don explained that the first two days would likely be about the prosecution and defense agreeing on a jury from a cattle call of potential candidates. He expected the trial to last a week. He was off by just one day.

Mom and I arrived at Don's office on a Monday an hour before the trial was to begin. We were seated in the lobby within earshot of a heated exchange between Jane and Don. I had grown accustomed to this over the past year but it was disturbing so close to the trial. Surely they had their act together by now. It was clear that Jane and Don didn't like each other much but there was a mutual respect between attorney and assistant that kept it from being personal. Any less would have constituted a hostile work environment. I was told that Don was a shark in the courtroom and a lawyer that you definitely wanted on your side. Despite all that had happened, it troubled me knowing a little girl was going to be raked over the coals by this man at some point during the week.

Don had suggested that I wear what was comfortable to me so I appeared in slacks and polo shirts. I had not eaten well or slept for days yet found myself incredibly focused as we entered the court room for jury selection. The game was afoot.

> *"Some people run from a possible fight*
> *Some people figure they can never win*
> *And although this is a fight I can lose*
> *The accused is an innocent man . . ."*
>
> Billy Joel, "An Innocent Man"

CHAPTER 20: WE, THE JURY . . .

Don entered the courtroom with a swagger. He frequently stood while his opposition sat. He knew people in the courtroom and acknowledged them with a smile I had rarely seen. It was his stage and we were all spectators lucky enough to have bought a ticket.

I had input into the selection of each juror but ultimately the prosecution had to agree before the individual was confirmed. It was late in the afternoon of day two when the final selection was made. Both Don and I were satisfied though not overly pleased with the finalists. Some seemed potentially sympathetic to the prosecution though we felt like there were a few in our corner as well.

Jury instructions and a brief address from Judge Parrish preceded opening statements and the calling of witnesses. Perhaps most telling was the absence of Alice's therapist for the past year and the social worker from Child Protective Services who conducted the initial intake interview just after the abuse report was filed. Each side summoned "expert" witnesses who ultimately did little to affect the outcome of the trial.

I sat quietly and stoically for two days and took notes on a legal pad, occasionally conferring with Don. During breaks, I chatted with Mom and many members of the First Christian Church who came to support us both. In fact, there was an entire gallery of friends and acquaintances who took time from personal commitments to be at my side. I was overwhelmed and humbled by their loyalty. These people believed in me. As a result, I became stronger just when I needed to be.

Jane made appearances in and out of the courtroom and prepared our witnesses. She was the ultimate stage manager in this legal melodrama that had captivated the local media and much of the community.

On the first day, Mom and I walked with Jane and others to a local eatery during the lunch break. Reporters from the three network affiliates and the Topeka Capital-Journal converged on us at the door. We brushed them aside and began the two block hike to the restaurant. Most backed away when we did not utter a statement, choosing to let their cameras capture the moment for the evening newscast. One reporter, however, stalked us as we quickened our pace towards the restaurant, while pestering Mom for a comment. Flustered, my 77 year old mother began to fall behind our group. I had not noticed until I heard her shriek "Leave me alone!" I had never heard such a frantic cry from her in my life. I quickly turned to charge the reporter but was restrained by my entourage. Mom soon caught up and order was restored.

A sheriff's deputy who had witnessed Mom's altercation with the reporter approached us upon our return. He respectfully asked if we would like an escort when entering or leaving the courthouse. I nodded politely and thanked him. From that day forward, we parked the car at Don's office and rode with Jane to the courthouse. Once at the courthouse, we were escorted inside through a basement tunnel. The sequence was repeated in the evening, as vehicles enabling the electronic media to do live remote broadcasts were stationed just east of the courthouse like buzzards waiting on a fence for a sick animal to die.

Father Pete and the school principal were witnesses for the prosecution but gave a favorable account of my time as the director of the Early Education Center. Angie was admittedly terrified but focused and confident when she took the stand. She proved to be a great asset to our defense. Glenda Jolly, another teacher, was also a star on the witness stand. Glenda had always been there for me both in and out of the workplace. Our friendship continues to this day and it is one I cherish.

Detective Lindquist proved to be a major liability for the prosecution just as I suspected he would. Don playfully insisted that my entire interrogation be heard by the jury despite the DA's desire to have it edited "for the sake of time" (it was more than two hours in length.) Clearly they wanted some of the detective's blunders erased. His beleaguered attempt to coerce a confession was met with chuckles from my gallery. At one point, an annoyed prosecutor objected and asked that the gallery be cleared from the courtroom. Judge Parrish reminded him that laughter was not so infuriating when in response to his carefully crafted witticisms earlier in the week. At that moment I felt some vindication after enduring that intolerable two plus hours with the bumbling detective.

The video resumed and painted a clear portrait of incompetence of one hell-bent but inexperienced detective. At one point, Don asked if he had contacted Yvonne in Arizona. The detective replied that he had called Yvonne. Don asked why that had not been mentioned in his official report. The reply was something to the effect of "I don't know."

At that point, Don reminded detective Lindquist that police procedure demanded that all contacts be logged. I suspected Lindquist and Yvonne were friends while she was a police officer. Naturally my suspicions were aroused when she told me that detective Lindquist had contacted her in Arizona. Yvonne was fired from the police department in 1997. How was it that the detective had her Arizona cell number after all these years?

Day four provided the moment I dreaded more than being called to witness stand myself: Alice was next to testify. The young prosecutor had finished his questioning and now it was time for the gloves to come off. It was at this moment that I gained an even greater respect for my attorney. His approach was warm and non-threatening. His questions benign but direct. Don wanted details of the day; details we knew the girl could not provide simply because she had fabricated the story; details that other investigators did not bother with to establish if this child was ever telling the truth.

What time of the day was it? What was she wearing? The specifics of this game we allegedly played and how often it happened. What did the room look like? And the $64,000 question—what shoes was I wearing. Over the course of a thirty minute cross examination, Alice responded "I don't know" 51 times to Don's barrage of questions.

On fifth and final day of testimony, it was my turn to take the stand in my own defense. Jane had prepared me well for Don's questions but I had no clue where the prosecution was going with his inquiries. Although drained from days of testimony and drama, I found myself remarkably composed and focused. Things seemed to be going our way although Don was too guarded to let on. I took the stand, gave my oath, and listened intently as the prosecutor asked questions I had answered a hundred times, beginning with detective Lindquist then later with Jane and Don.

For months I had imagined the prosecution trying to produce inconsistencies in my story through a maze of questions phrased eighteen different ways over several hours. Within ten minutes he was finished. Don gave me a wry smile as he stood and clarified key points of my testimony. He then asked what shoes I wore that day.

"The shoes I have on today," I replied.

He asked me to show the court and I stuck my size 13's out for all to see. Slip-on leather casuals. No strings attached. I was dismissed and returned to my seat for the closing arguments.

By now it was 4:30 on Friday and the jury was instructed to begin its deliberations. A verdict had not been reached by 5:30 and Judge Parrish sent the weary jurors home for the weekend. Deliberations would resume Monday morning. My fate was put on hold through what was the longest weekend of my life.

The next two days were like an out-of-body experience. I was somewhat aware of the moment but my mind was racing at warp speed and a thousand scenarios were playing out in my mind. If I were declared innocent, I would go home and pack for an Arizona road trip to see Josh. If guilty, it would become necessary to settle my affairs in the event I was taken directly into custody. Don was not sure how it would play out and suggested I be prepared. The latter sent an icy chill through my body and the thought of a guilty verdict haunted me throughout the weekend just as it had done for the past year.

Needing something to do, I volunteered to help good friend Brian Hettrick move his mother-in-law into a new home in Kansas City. Brian was a reformed hell raiser and retired skydiver with more than 1,300 jumps to his credit.

By now I was pale and emaciated. My weight had dropped from 220 to 178 pounds. Brian had known me since our college days at Kansas State. He told me months later that I looked like death when I showed up in front of the U-Haul truck.

In addition to the weight loss, muscle atrophy had set in. By no means could I have ever been mistaken for Hulk Hogan but I did work out and at least had some tone to my body. My exercise regimen was limited to walks with Dixie and hopping roof tops with Phil. I was almost unrecognizable to friends and struggled to lift pieces of heavy furniture into the house. However, the day with Brian and his family did provide a temporary respite from the trial and I was grateful for that.

Monday arrived and I was confident that the jury would come to a final decision by day's end. I was not disappointed. Though surrounded by my band of supporters from the church, work, and one incredibly devoted mother, I secluded myself to ponder a fate that would be decided in mere moments. Don came to get me. We were being summoned back to court. The jury had only taken 45 minutes to reach a verdict.

The jury foreman stood.

"We the jury find the defendant, Timothy Thomas McHenry, *not guilty*."

A shriek could be heard (I think it was Mom) followed by cheers and applause. My head fell to into my hands and I wept uncontrollably for what seemed to be minutes before raising my head and turning back to my gallery with grateful acknowledgement. I felt Don's arm on my shoulder followed by a congratulatory handshake as he gathered his papers and placed them in his briefcase.

Judge Parrish had allowed the media in the courtroom for the reading of the verdict. It was the first time they had access to the proceedings. Within minutes, I was squinting through camera lights. For the first time, reporters were polite and asked if I would answer some questions once I had composed myself. I agreed and responded to a few harmless inquiries lobbed my way and then entered the hall to what was like a receiving line at a wedding. Hugs and well wishes abounded. Several of us decided it was time for breakfast and agreed to meet at the IHOP just down the street from the courthouse.

Finally I saw Jane who had been working tirelessly on my behalf for the past year. She was as giddy as a school girl. We embraced and privately celebrated our victory. Jane told me that Judge Parrish wanted to see me. The judge was standing just outside her chambers and was smiling as I approached.

"You handled yourself well this week," she said. "And I just wanted to wish you the best."

"Thank you, Your Honor, for everything," I replied softly.

I was utterly speechless in her presence. Judge Parrish was true to her profession. She called it down the middle. I could not have asked for more.

Don declined the invitation to breakfast. He had already moved onto the next stage where he would no doubt give a command performance. Jane marched my posse to the restaurant and for the first time in nearly a week, I enjoyed a meal. I ordered French toast and I savored every bite.

Each day as I seated myself before Judge Parrish, I placed two photographs of Josh and me on the table next to my legal pad. I needed something concrete to keep me grounded amidst the surreal backdrop of the trial. There was a third picture, that of Dixie. To some, it may sound unusual, even bizarre, to draw strength from an animal. But Dixie wasn't just any animal nor was Josh just some kid. They, along with Mom, were the loves of my life. Josh was (is) a miracle whose life I have been privileged to share. Sadly, our time together has been all too brief. Though I am credited with rescuing Dixie, her presence begs the question "who saved whom?" Dixie had given me something she had lost a year ago, a leg to stand on. How could anyone not draw strength from that?

Melissa Brunner was the news anchor of Topeka's CBS affiliate that produced the video of Dixie and me for the Helping Hands Humane Society benefit in 2006. I found her to be quite different than most media types I had met over the years. She was down to earth, sensitive, funny, and committed to her community. We both exercised at the YWCA fitness center while I served as that agency's youth services director. Josh often waited in the lobby while I hustled through my routine. One day, Melissa postponed her exercise session to play with Josh while I finished my workout. I never forgot that act of kindness and told her as much when we met a few months before the trial.

"When this ordeal is over, regardless of how it turns out, I'll talk to you first," I said.

Don phoned a couple hours after the verdict. Melissa had called him and asked to interview the two of us. He wanted to know if I was up to it. Though already exhausted from the day's events, I remembered my promise to her and agreed. The questions reflected compassion and insight. I chose my words carefully so as to avoid unleashing the rage I felt about all that my family and friends had been through.

That segment was the lead story on the 6 and 10 p.m. newscasts. The other guys had to settle for my brief comments after the verdict had been read. There was a time where I used the media to promote Big Brothers/Big Sisters and became quite comfortable in front of a microphone or camera. After today, I knew I would never want to see my mug on a TV screen or in a newspaper ever again. Now that it was over, I just wanted to disappear into utter anonymity.

*"For just a Skyline Pigeon
Dreaming of the open, waiting for the day
He can spread his wings and fly away again . . ."*

Elton John/Bernie Taupin, "Skyline Pigeon"

CHAPTER 21: VINDICATION

The following day, I loaded Dixie into the car and headed for Prescott, AZ. I had never felt so free. With my favorite traveling companion, we drove through the golden wheat fields of western Kansas along Interstate 70, then across the plains of eastern Colorado and into Denver for the night just as before.

The drive takes about 24 hours, the equivalent of two hard days on the road. I make pit stops about every four hours to shake the cobwebs while Dixie romps and takes care of business. Somehow I always managed to find a baseball field in some small town just off the highway that we converted into our personal dog park. It amazes me that we haven't been run off by some anal retentive groundskeeper wielding a weed whacker in one hand and a Louisville Slugger® in the other.

Besides seeing Josh, my favorite part of the trip is the mountains. Few of Mother Earth's natural wonders compare to the Rockies and I-70 carves through the southernmost corner. We take in scenic views and short nature walks as we travel west, always wishing the day was just a bit longer so that we could inhale the crisp mountain air just one more time. Dixie loves the mountains and navigates them as if she were a bighorn sheep. She is truly in her element and I feel I am too when surrounded by jagged peaks that majestically tower over the horizon. One day I will live in such a place. For now, we will just have to settle for the title of tourist.

Once west of the Rockies, we pass through Grand Junction, Colorado and venture into Utah. It is nearly time to abandon the four-lane in favor of state highways that take us south through the always spectacular Monument Valley National Park. Sadly, most of our national parks don't allow dogs out of the car so we seek out state parks with plenty of hiking trails friendly to both critters with two, three, or four legs. South of Monument Valley are the Indian reservations where our country has conveniently managed to warehouse an entire civilization of people.

Winslow, AZ, made famous in the song "Take It Easy" by the Eagles, is where we pick up Interstate 40 and head west into Flagstaff, then south across the Mingus Mountains into Prescott. It is familiar terrain, as I lived in this picturesque mountain community for several years.

I have often found long rides in the car to be tedious and ultimately uncomfortable as I crumple my 6'4" frame into whatever I am driving for hours on end. Still, it beats the heck out of air travel with its security protocols and insufferable delays. In the car I am on my time. I stop when I want to take in the splendor of this great country. Best of all, I get to ride with my dog.

Dixie could not be a better traveling companion. Ironically, she shows no fear of a contraption that turned her left front leg into hamburger. I open the door and she hops effortlessly aboard her chariot and onto a waiting dog bed without a care as to our final destination. I traded my clunker for a Honda Element which is essentially a dog kennel on wheels. Others have referred to it as a rolling toaster but it serves my needs without fail. Occasionally Dixie looks out the window or peers into the front seat for some affection and I gladly reciprocate. Unlike some dogs, Dixie requires no barriers to keep her off my lap, nor has she ever succumbed to motion sickness. For us, the ride is about being together and rejoicing in whatever adventure we are about to share.

After getting settled for the night, Dixie and I picked up Josh at his mother's current place of employment. We embraced and Josh immediately asked about the trial once we climbed into the truck.

"I was acquitted," I replied knowing that I had already told his mother this.

"That means you didn't do it, right Dad?"

"Yes, son, that means I didn't do it."

"Cool," was all he said and we went to lunch.

Neither of us spoke of the trial again until the final day. While hiking the Granite Mountain Trail, I tried to impart just what had been at stake during this trial and how incredibly stressful the experience had been. Although Josh was nearly 14 now, I was not confident that he could grasp the enormity of it all. I wanted him to understand that being his dad, even from 1,200 miles away, kept me grounded throughout the harrowing week of the trial. The images of him and Dixie that accompanied me to court each day served as a harbor in the tempest that was my life.

I was disappointed to hear that Josh's grades had plummeted to the point where he was failing most of his classes. It wasn't so much a lack of understanding as it was effort. Josh had shut down. He confessed that he wasn't taking the medication prescribed to treat his ADHD. He hadn't swam or played music since he left Kansas. From where I stood, Josh was slipping into an adolescent black hole.

Although our visit was a pleasant one, I left Prescott with a heavy heart knowing there was little I could do 1,200 miles removed. Regrets filled my head as Dixie and I made our way back to Kansas. If only I had not let him go in the first place. Dammit! Then again, he would have suffered through the accusation and subsequent trial just like the rest of us. Was he, in fact, better off in the vacuum of his mother's care in Arizona?

Josh seemed to have no reservations about letting me in the house this time. The single-wide mobile home reeked of dog urine from Yvonne's ill-mannered Chihuahuas. In fact, one of them defecated on the floor in Josh's room while we sat together discussing the latest "Harry Potter" book.

"It happens all the time," Josh said. I'll get it later."

Our time grew short and I was again faced with the unpleasantness of goodbye. At least I would be seeing him for Christmas in just two short months and then again the following spring. We hiked up a Prescott landmark known as Thumb Butte during our last hours together. Josh fancied himself an amateur photographer and took pictures with a disposable camera. We dropped off the camera at Walgreens and had the pictures back in an hour. His pictures weren't half bad from what I know of photography. As Dixie and I drove back to Overland Park, I could not help but think that I had unearthed one more talent that would never be realized as long as he lived in the great cultural Mecca known as Chino Valley, Arizona.

"You thought you could find happiness
Just over that green hill
You thought you would be satisfied
But you never will learn to be still . . ."
Don Henley/Stanley Lynch, *"Learn To Be Still"*

CHAPTER 22: PRODIGAL SONS

It was time to reclaim my job with PetSmart. During the company-imposed sabbatical, I had tried to contact anyone involved in Human Resources for an explanation as to why I was unable to work prior to a verdict being rendered. Phone messages were not returned. I even stopped by the corporate office in Phoenix before visiting Josh a year ago and asked if I could talk some someone about my plight. The receptionist apparently was not accustomed to associates from Kansas walking in off the street without an appointment and nervously said there was no one available.

"That's OK, I'll wait," and I sat down in the lobby with a magazine.

About an hour later, two young security guards informed that I was not going to be talking with anyone from HR and politely asked that I leave. Their tone suggested some urgency to the request and so I reluctantly complied. What a story for the gang back home. I was unceremoniously thrown out of the corporate office. There was apparently no opportunity for appeal.

"Whatever happened to "innocent until proven guilty?" I wondered.

Evidently that applies only in the courtroom. Not so under the microscope of the media and in the board room. It was one of many lessons I took from this experience.

To PetSmart's credit, they were true to their word. I was given the green light and returned to work as a pet trainer. Both Vince and Jennifer welcomed me back with open arms as did my fellow associates who were told that I had taken time off for personal reasons. I did not elaborate nor did they ask which was fine by me. Life was beginning to return to what was a new state of normalcy.

For the most part, I chose not to socialize with my workmates. They were a good lot but I had become intensely private since the accusation. The gregarious, animated, camera mugging bloke from my past had become reserved, unobtrusive and wanting nothing more than to blend into the scenery. Old friendships and a wonderful dog named Dixie would quench my need for companionship.

Dustin Leonard was the one exception. He began his career at PetsMart as a cashier and was quickly promoted to a department manager. We had exchanged friendly banter, mostly about sports. One night, word came that there was to be a massive pet food recall. Vince asked for volunteers to stay late and remove the affected products from the shelves and inventory them. Dustin and I both signed on and worked side by side until 3 a.m.

We had virtually nothing in common. I was a card carrying Democrat with a social agenda. He was a distant right of the political fifty yard line. My faith in the Christian God I grew up with was fading while Dustin was a Nazarene. He was 21. I was older than his father. Yet out of that kettle of divergent views came a friendship that has sustained the Bush and Obama administrations. To this day, we meet weekly for lunch and occasionally venture into the movie theatre or disc golf course. Dustin is mature beyond his years. The eldest of five, he also cared for his younger siblings, fixed his own car, and was as self-sufficient as any young person I had ever met.

Dustin has cerebral palsy which makes him all the more remarkable. For the time being, he has limited use of his right foot and walks with a noticeable limp. Today he is the assistant manager of a small hardware chain and spends most of the day on his feet. He is married now and is expecting a son. Dustin will make a wonderful father.

It was my turn to have Josh for the Christmas holidays and it wound up being a relatively inexpensive investment on my part, as he hitched a ride with his stepfather who was returning to visit relatives. I never had much use for the men that Yvonne had dated over the years, as few offered little more than casual indifference towards my son. Charles was different. When he learned that neither Josh nor his mother had done any holiday shopping for Grandma or me, Charles stopped a Topeka K-Mart so that Josh could pick out gifts. He then purchased wrapping paper and insisted that Josh present his purchases in the spirit of the season. Charles had earned my respect that day and I am pleased that he is a part of my son's life.

We always go to church with Grandma and Josh's appearance at the Sunday service was nothing short of a celebration for the prodigal son. We were both members of the First Christian Church in Topeka. Like me, very few members had actually begun their faith journey with First Christian. Josh, however, was dedicated and eventually baptized there. He was popular among the adults as well as the youth so his return was met with much hoopla. Rev. Jim even scooped him up as though he was re-enacting the service where Josh was dedicated into the church as an infant. Though slightly embarrassed, Josh basked in the moment and I secretly hoped such a homecoming might inspire him to give us another try. This was not to be the case and the holiday ended with me driving Josh through an early winter blizzard to meet up with Charles and return to sunny Arizona.

"Well it's comin' together I finally feel like a man
I never thought that I'd be where I am
Every day I wake a little bit higher
I keep pushin' on . . ."
REO Speedwagon, "Keep Pushin'"

CHAPTER 23: A CHINK IN THE ARMOR

Shortly after turning the calendar to 2008, the position of "area trainer" came open at PetSmart and I leaped at the opportunity. Not only was this a promotion but the job would enable me to teach what I had learned to new trainers hired by the company. Actually, there were two "area trainer" postings. Angelique was chosen for the first position. I was selected for the second. The district services manager did not want two area trainers in the same store and so one of us had to transfer. Angelique had seniority by a few months and she chose to remain in Olathe which meant it was time for me to move on.

Just a short drive east was a PetSmart store in Overland Park. It featured a Pets Hotel which was something new to my PetSmart experience. My classes were taught in a room set aside for a doggie day camp program. A Plexiglas® wall gave me full view of the sales floor. Customers would frequently stop to watch classes in session which made me feel like a Sea World exhibit.

The store manager was an experienced retailer named Kathy Allen. Unlike many PetSmart store managers, Kathy truly loved animals and dogs were her favorite. She was the guardian of two pampered Poodles that got the very best her retail salary could offer. I quickly discovered that Kathy was also a talker which is like saying that Michael Jordan occasionally played basketball. She was tagged "Chatty Kathy" by several associates. It didn't take long to see why.

Part of my business plan involved using Dixie as a "demo" dog, meaning that she would walk the sales floor with me in search of customers needing pet training solutions. I winced at the idea of exploiting her disability to promote sales but also knew that the primary reason pet owners relinquish their dogs is due to behavior issues. If Dixie's presence kept one dog in its home and not discarded at a local shelter, so much the better. The end certainly justified the means.

By now Dixie had repertoire tricks like push-ups, rolling over, waiting for a treat that rested on her front paw, catching a treat that balanced precariously on her nose, crawl, bow, and spin, just to name a few. My favorites were the multiple choice game that required her to wait patiently while I laid four treats on the floor and cued her to wait. After a pause, Dixie then picks them up one at a time as I give the release command. Customers would stop to catch our little vaudeville act which was a great transition into a discussion about training.

Another was the infamous "play dead." How twisted is this? I would pretend to shoot my dog with my finger while saying "bang-bang." Dixie took this cue and would roll over on her side into what's known as the "settle" position. I turned around as if to walk away, then "shot" her a few more times which cued a roll to the back with her one leg extended upward, a sort of canine rigor mortis that delighted even the most upstanding of Overland Park customers.

Finally, there was our adaptation of "shake" where, upon command, Dixie would roll over and place her right paw into my hand. Suffice to say that teaching a dog with three legs "shake" in the traditional way would result in a few broken teeth so adjustments had to be made.

During my days at PetSmart, Dixie and I were privileged to work the grand openings of new stores where she basked in the glow of the spotlight whenever it shined upon her. PetSmart occasionally sponsored community events promoting the adoption of pets. This often meant handing out information and do-dads from a booth and Dixie was all too happy to oblige. She also maintained morale at associate meetings as well as seminars that I conducted for my colleagues as an area trainer.

Besides teaching my own classes, PetSmart began sending recent hires to me for the same two week academy I had attended in Independence. Time would be spent learning about canine ethology, genetics, how dogs communicate and learn, classroom management, and sales. On top of that, the new hire's dog handling and teaching skills would be assessed.

Somehow two weeks didn't seem enough to do justice to those subjects given that many trainers spend months earning certifications through nationally recognized organizations and accredited colleges. A two week academy with a trainer who had only been on the job for just over a year seemed inadequate but this was the task before me and I had accepted the challenge when promoted to the position of area trainer. Besides, it added "guinea pig" to Dixie's ever expanding PetSmart job description. Now my students had a real dog to sharpen the same dog handling skills they would be expecting their own students to learn. Over the years I have found that this experience separated the serious trainers from the wannabes.

At the risk of sounding anthropomorphic, Dixie opted for the role of ornery student. While with students, she will pull ahead during a loose leash walking or heel drill, break out of a sit/stay and run towards Kathy's office in search of treats, or anticipate the trainees' request and flop into a down before the cue is given. Secretly it was laughable and nearly brought weaker students to their knees.

It occurred to me that this wonderful dog not only inspired me but brought a smile to anyone who noticed her unusual gait. Dixie had become a bit of a mascot for the group of stores that comprised our district. She had a job and it is my belief that every dog needs a job. With that, I began to explore other opportunities to enrich her life. It was the least I could do after all that she had given to me the past two years.

PetSmart helped to create a new identity for me. Because I was one of two associates sporting the name of "Tim," I had become "Tim the Trainer." In fact, I started signing certificates of completion for my students with that very nameplate. It gave me a certain degree of comfortable anonymity even though my last name was printed on business cards that I handed out like candy throughout my PetSmart day. My reputation, not to mention my career, would be doomed if anyone became too curious as to why a 48 year old man abandoned the career for which he was trained to suddenly became a dog trainer.

I needed a cover story. With each new class, I explained that adopting Dixie was one of the most powerful experiences of my life. When my son moved away in 2006, I had an opportunity to change careers. I have a teaching background so dog training was the obvious choice. That was my story and I stuck with it. For the most part, it was the truth. In reality, I became a dog trainer because I could no longer be an early education center director. I was still a "substantiated" child abuser in the eyes of Child Protective Services and no court verdict could reverse that finding. In all likelihood, I would never work with children again. This was hardly the biography I would share with my students.

One day in the summer of 2008, Dixie sat politely at my side while I talked with a mother, her young daughter, and their new Boxer puppy. As I explained the virtues of early training, the child became restless, picked up her puppy, and began dropping the frightened little animal on top of Dixie's head. I uttered an uncomfortable "oops, be careful" while Mom continued to ignore the behavior. Dixie was tolerant at first but then became increasingly agitated, trying to avoid the falling puppy by shifting one way then the other. Finally, she let loose a *"stop that, dammit!"* guttural growl and the girl began to cry. The mother immediately withdrew with child in hand and the puppy clinging precariously to the daughter's shoulder.

"That dog is mean," she exclaimed as they retreated to file a complaint with management.

Dixie and I bailed to the break room. I was furious on two fronts: First, at the parent who was oblivious to her child's behavior and the care of the puppy; secondly, I was angry at myself. Fearful of losing the sale, I did not intervene on Dixie's behalf. This was only the beginning of a pattern of behavior I found most disconcerting. Dixie was becoming reactive to other dogs.

My own training had not prepared me for this. I scoffed at the notion that the trainer could not manage his own dog. How hypocritical was that?

Or maybe I was just over reacting. Surely this was not to be a pattern but an isolated incident. Sadly, the former played out in spades over the next several months.

Three incidents at the dog parks over the years served to throw gas on Dixie's reactivity fire. Each one involved Boxers or Boxer/American Bulldog mixes. Though sweet and sensitive by nature, these dogs tend to be a bit rambunctious at play and Dixie would have no part in that unless she was familiar with the dog. While living with Phil, Dixie and the goofy Golden Retriever Cody would play doggie mosh pit for what seemed like hours on end.

An overzealous boxer T-boned Dixie at Topeka's Bark Park about a year ago, sending her sprawling across the grass and momentarily knocking the wind out of her sails. She struggled to her feet only to be submarined by the same dog. The force of the collision flipped her over like a box turtle in the middle of the highway. Dixie landed with a thud. It was the first time I had heard her yelp. I was several yards away and ran to her defense but the boxer has already zeroed in on another unsuspecting target while the handler stood by haplessly calling her dog.

There have been two similar incidents at Stoll Park over four years, both involving boxers. One left Dixie bleeding from the jowls. She became more reactive with each incident, especially towards any dog that even resembled a boxer or was big enough to stand over her. She barely noticed smaller dogs and loved Maggie, my mother's Dachshund. She remained friends with Phil's dogs Cody and Katie. With the approach of a boxer or facsimile thereof, Dixie developed this *"I'm gonna get you before you get me"* mindset that was impossible to diffuse because she never snapped until the dog was right up in her grill. Intervention therefore became difficult. Dixie was more reactive on leash but she could be equally grumpy off leash.

This much was certain: The behavior was clearly fear based. As a trainer, I knew that Dixie's days as a demonstration dog were on hold until I could get a handle on this. For now, I needed to find Dixie another job and find a way to help my troubled girl.

Patricia McConnell published what has been my blueprint for dealing Dixie's problem. It's called "Feisty Fido: Help for the Leash Reactive Dog." She is now my personal training guru. I started Dixie on a treatment plan utilizing desensitizing and counter-conditioning techniques detailed in the book. Much to my dismay, I learned that my reactions to an approaching dog were part of the problem. As a result, I have learned some techniques that help both Dixie and me relax at the approach of another dog. From there, it was basically a matter of changing Dixie's perception of other dogs by giving her something else to do and rewarding her generously for it. While she has made improvements, she can still be reactive if another dog makes a sudden move towards her while in her personal space so there is still much work to be done.

"We've been through some things together
With trunks of memories still to come
We found things to do in stormy weather
Long may you run..."

Neil Young, *"Long May You Run"*

CHAPTER 24: CLEAN RUNNING

In April, hundreds of vendors and thousands of dog enthusiasts descend upon a local sports/concert venue for the Kansas City Pet Expo. For me, it was the World Series and Super Bowl all rolled into one weekend. I felt like one of those groupies at a Star Trek convention as I entered the cavernous hall. There were breed specific rescue groups, local shelters with dogs to adopt, and vendors hawking everything from canine massage to funeral packages.

What caught my eye were the exhibitions. Of course there were the police dogs mauling some poor cop in a padded suit. Been there, seen that.

There was this crazy relay game called "fly ball" where frenzied teams jumped over hurdles, punched a button on a box to release a tennis ball, and then returned to the starting line with the ball secured in their mouth where another member of the team would repeat the exercise.

Most of the dogs were terriers whose barking reached a fever pitch as they awaited their turn to retrieve the tennis ball. Owners and handlers would add to the mayhem by screaming at their dogs to "hurry" as if they needed any encouragement in that department. It was clearly an adrenalin rush for all involved but I was certain that the sheer volume would overwhelm my noise sensitive pooch. If I were to draw a cartoon of an energy drink convention, it would look something like fly ball.

Dock diving. Now that was cool. The recipe is pretty straightforward, even for this kitchen klutz. One part dog, about 50 feet of dock, and a pinch of tennis ball or other retrieving toy, then add water. Lots of water. Dog sits on one end of the platform and runs towards the handler stationed at the far end dangling the item to be retrieved. It's all about timing. When dog reaches maximum velocity, the toy is tossed out over a pool of water and the frantic dog goes airborne. The distance from the platform to splashdown is measured and the longest launch wins. Imagine being on the runway when the Concord takes off and you get the idea. I dreamed of Dixie as a four legged dock diving champ but that was not to be her fate.

I had seen agility trials on Animal Planet. The sport of canine agility is like an obstacle course for dogs. The goal is for the dog to complete a course featuring 13-20 various obstacles as quickly as possible. There are tunnels, tires suspended a couple of feet off the ground, hoops, hurdles, a teeter-totter, weaves, an A-frame, and ramps that support a balance beam several feet off the ground. The obstacles are sequential and a dog is judged based on the successful navigation of each one.

The "Bark Park" in Topeka had a couple of tunnels and jumps. One day, Dixie jumped on top of a steel tunnel while playing with another dog. At this point, I had only begun to realize her potential. Dixie had already shown her athleticism while navigating the rocks at Arizona's Granite Dells. Teaching her to run through the tunnel and jump through a tire was accomplished in about 20 minutes so I knew even then we were onto something. Bark Park patrons were in awe over this dog with a missing leg that could plow through a tunnel and leap like a gazelle. So graceful was Dixie that most onlookers were unaware that she had three legs until she stopped to collect her reward then peeled through the maze all over again.

An agility course had been laid out at the Pet Expo and I tore myself away from dock diving to check it out. I stood fascinated as handlers skillfully directed their dogs through the obstacles and knew that this was the sport for us. I spoke with a volunteer following the exhibition who directed me to a website listing upcoming classes. Although I worked Sundays, Saturdays were mine and we enrolled in a morning class with a very competent instructor named Sharon.

There are many challenging obstacles comprising an agility course. Tunnels resemble an oversized version of that plastic tubing that connects to the back of your clothes dryer and vents hot air into the atmosphere. I suspect politicians keep extras on hand when they hit the campaign trail. Tunnels extend to lengths of twenty feet or so and can be bent like a horseshoe which makes them more challenging when the dog can no longer see daylight at the end.

Hoops are nothing more than Hula Hoops® anchored to a frame. In one agility event, handlers are required to lead their dogs through each one in the proper sequence.

Then there are the elusive weave poles. Each is between 41 and 48 inches in height. They are set in a line of six or 12 and are 18 or 24 inches apart. Dogs are trained to slink in and out of the weave poles with the precision of an Olympic gymnast.

Two obstacles test a dog's balance and climbing ability. These are referred to as the "contacts." One is simply an elevated table that a dog at full throttle must stop, lie down, and stay for five seconds before proceeding to another obstacle. Another contact involves two wooden platforms set upright and hinged together in the shape of the letter "A." The "contact" is usually painted a bright color at the base of each platform. The dog must touch the colored area on the way up and again on the way down. It is referred to as an "A-frame."

Another contact looks like a balance beam used by female gymnasts. Again, the dog must touch the contact on the way up a ramp, cross the narrow beam, and touch the contact as she descends. Agility aficionados call it the "walk-it."

Hurdles are set up throughout the course. The height of the bar can range from four to 26 inches depending on the size of the dog. Some courses even have tires suspended above the ground for the dogs to jump through.

It was evident a few minutes into the first class that Dixie was a natural. Best of all, she loved doing it. Agility combined four things near and dear to Dixie; running, climbing, food and me. We started with jumps and tunnels.

Once she cleared the hurdle, I clicked to mark the correct behavior while a treat lie in wait. If she bypassed the hurdle, the treat was withdrawn. Hoops and tires were eventually added and she conquered them in no time.

Tunnels were but a few feet in length in the beginning. I simply gestured by pushing my hand toward the entry of the tunnel then tapped the top to maintain her focus. Again, click and treat as she exited the tunnel. Soon, the tunnel was stretched out between 10 and 20 feet. Dixie rumbled through the tunnel like water through a garden hose. Eventually, the tunnel was angled and the exit was no longer in view. This was a different matter. In the beginning, she made a U-turn and exited while I stood haplessly by at the other end. It proved to only be a temporary setback once she realized that the food was only available by passing through the entire tunnel. Dixie could solve a Rubik's Cube™ if there was food involved.

Contacts were a bit of a challenge for Dixie. She needed a running start to scale the A-frame and missed the first contact. Once she reached the apex, she began her descent but leaped to the floor rather than touch the contact. Dixie approached each obstacle with such gusto that it was really a matter of just slowing her down. I was concerned that this might put undue stress on her front leg but Dixie seemed no worse for the wear. Still, the contacts remain a challenge to this day.

Our second series of classes focused on the confounded weave poles. These proved to be the most troublesome for Dixie. We discovered that a fourth leg comes in real handy when trying to snake through a set of six poles. To make matters worse, our days in agility classes with Sharon were unknowingly numbered.

Sharon invited us out to her outdoor practice facility in the small community of Louisburg located just south of Overland Park. Dixie had never run outdoors before and the all the enticing smells of farm country proved to be more than distracting. As we practiced, I paused to let Dixie take in these wonderful odors and asked Sharon if she thought Dixie was ready to compete as a novice in a sanctioned competition. She gave us her blessing along with the website of the North American Dog Agility Council, a/k/a NADAC. Sharon felt this organization would be more receptive to Dixie's participation than the American Kennel Club.

As it turned out, NADAC would allow Dixie to compete but only in non-jumping events; in short, no hurdles or contacts. We would be restricted to competition, that contained only hoops, tunnels, and/or weaves. I contacted our wonderful veterinarian Dr. Jed Barnes at Bradford Animal Hospital who laughed at the notion that Dixie was a liability risk and wrote a letter in support of her participation. I mailed the letter with my appeal to the NADAC powers that be but the initial ruling was upheld. Dixie could only enter competitions where her three paws were grounded. This ruling did not govern practice sessions so we continued to train on all the equipment. Ironically, NADAC hosts events for handlers with disabilities.

Begrudgingly, I accepted NADAC's decision, knowing this would likely be the only governing body that would allow Dixie to do what she loved outside of a classroom experience. To satisfy my curiosity, I contacted the AKC and was told Dixie would not be allowed to participate at any level of agility due to her "disability." Sharon was right. We registered for a NADAC sanctioned competition to be held in Lawrence, KS over the Memorial Day Weekend in 2009.

About a week after submitting our registration, I received an e-mail from Sharon stating that she was "no longer comfortable" training Dixie and that my class fee would be refunded. She apologized without stating the reason for our expulsion and it puzzles me to this day. Was it the NADAC limitations or the AKC ruling? Did she catch the "liability fever?" Or did a Google search of my recent past make me a leper in her eyes?

I continued to refer my PetSmart students to Sharon if they expressed interest in agility, as I found her to be an outstanding instructor. I didn't see this coming and I hurt for Dixie, who so very much loved this sport. But we were registered for a "tunnelers" competition in a few weeks and dammit if we weren't going to turn some heads.

Going to an agility trial reminded me of the first time I walked into Starbucks. The language they were speaking was English but I could decipher little beyond that. We didn't know a "Q" (qualifying run) from a Skinny Dolce Crème Frappuccino (I still don't know what that the hell that is). So we sat. And we listened. And we asked.

We learned that there are three divisions—elite, open, and novice. No question that we were novices. Even though Dixie was not allowed to jump, we still had to enter at a certain jump height loosely based on the dog's measurement at the withers. She would compete in the novice division head-to-head with other dogs at that jump height. For Dixie, that was 16 inches.

After competing, her time would be posted next to a column marked "standard course time." This was the average time to complete the course. To earn qualifying points that would eventually enable us to earn a title and move up into the next division, Dixie had to run under the standard course time not just once but three times.

The trial was held 45 minutes to the west at the fairgrounds in Lawrence, Kansas. It was a tad stuffy, as the trial was held indoors over the Memorial Day weekend in a horse arena. The building had no air conditioning. The dirt surface made running the course feel a little like plodding through kitty litter.

Contestants were allowed to walk the course to choreograph their own movements so as to successfully navigate their dog from one obstacle to another. Dogs were not allowed on the course until it was their time to compete. Hand gestures are often used to maneuver the dogs and watching us move about the course without our dogs must have resembled a convention of traffic cops.

The judge gave us about 10 minutes to walk the course and I took the full allotment of time. There were 17 passes through various tunnels scattered throughout the arena. As I walked, I felt myself enter that "zone" that reminded me of my competitive days on the ball diamond just minutes before a pitching assignment. My heart rate increased, the adrenalin glands were on stand-by, and all expression left my face.

"This is just for fun," I kept telling myself.

But the competitive juices that I thought had long since been silenced suddenly emerged. Dixie waited patiently in the car while I walked the course once last time. OK, well not so patiently, as her raspy high pitched "where are you?" bark could be heard from inside the arena. I retrieved

Dixie, who bounded out of the car with her game face on. While we waited our turn to run, she nervously chomped at the bit like a prize race horse at the starting gate.

The veteran competitors had cheerfully briefed us on ring etiquette and I was thankful for their advice. Dixie was to enter the ring with no collar. I could not have any training treats in view of the judge. Most competitors used a simple slip lead. Once in the ring, the leash remained on until the judge said "good luck." You could then start at any point.

I looked to the judge for the "good luck" cue and noticed that the ring was surrounded by fans and curious competitors who had apparently never seen a dog with three legs run an agility course. Many had asked if we were there to watch.

"No, we're here kick your ass."

Alright, so I was not so brazen, but I did make it clear that Dixie was no spectator.

"Good luck" pronounced the judge and I slid Dixie's lead over her head and tossed it to a waiting volunteer who would meet me at the end of the course. I placed Dixie in a sit, and gave her the "wait" cue. Then I released her.

Dixie charged through the tunnels like a hound dog tracking an escaped convict. Her eyes were on me and I knew I would have to move quickly to stay ahead of her. Unlike those competitors featured on "Animal Planet," we were not to the point where I could simply stand in the middle of the course and point to each tunnel. I had to commit Dixie to each one through a series of gestures without touching her or the tunnel itself.

It was about midway through the course that I erred. Dogs are rarely at fault when mistakes are made in agility or any other training exercise. It's a matter of the handler failing to properly communicate the next move. Such was the case here. I failed to commit Dixie to a tunnel before moving onto the next one. As a result, she veered away from the entry point and followed me. I quickly pivoted and redirected her to the tunnel opening. Dixie entered and then moved successfully through the remaining tunnels.

The joy on her face defied description. She loved agility. And most of all, I learned, Dixie loved to perform. We raced through the last tunnel and across the electronic sensor that recorded her time. I called Dixie to me and she jumped so high upon my chest that her right front leg touched me at the shoulder.

To my amazement there were cheers. Not just polite "golf" claps but rousing applause. Dixie spun several times and barked in acknowledgement as laughter filled the arena. Out of the corner of my eye I could see the judge and the scribe that kept the records smiling as we exited the course. My heart was racing and a measure of pride came over me that I had not felt in years. We WERE the moment for all the right reasons and not because of some lame accusation, venomous blog post or courtroom drama.

I sat in my lawn chair outside the arena and waited for the results to be posted. Dixie was still panting from the run but her mouth was turned upward towards a smile only a dog lover recognizes. Several minutes, later, I walked Dixie up to the scoring table. SECOND PLACE!!! Due to my mistake, it was not a qualifying run but that didn't matter. Dixie, in her first run, had earned a ribbon.

I reached in a storage drawer marked "second place ribbons" and picked out a bright red one, then collapsed back into my chair in an emotional heap. Tears of joy welled up in my eyes as I stroked Dixie's baby soft fur. Spectators and competitors alike came by to congratulate us and I tried to acknowledge each one. Public displays of emotion are not common for me but today it did not matter. Dixie had just given me one of the most amazing moments of my life and I wanted everyone to know just how proud I was of this amazing dog. Veterans of this sport will tell you that ribbons are nothing to write home about. It's the qualifying runs that matter. For us, the ribbon was both a culmination and a metaphor for things to come.

INSIGHTS: MY FAVORITE THINGS

Like any dog worth his weight in kibble, the center of my universe is the person I live with. His name is Tim. Some dogs live with a pack of humans but they usually have a favorite. I am for Tim. His happiness and safety are everything to me. Life without Tim would be worse than a Kong® without peanut butter. It just wouldn't make sense.

I've been so terribly worried about Tim since I came back from Angie's house. He rarely smiles. His walk has slowed and his eyes look only at the ground. The only time I smell joy is when we are doing something together so I never leave his side when he is home. Tim goes to work at the pet store in the middle of the day and does not return until it is dark outside. My job has no beginning, no end. It started the day he brought me home from the shelter and will continue long after I leave this body.

Tim and I are an agility team. We practice every week with four other dogs named Duke, Gideon, Odin and Marley. Duke is the biggest. I'm not sure, but he might be a horse. He likes to run off course but lately he's been doing much better. I'm quite certain that Odin is a horse and makes the A-frame buckle as he slowly walks up and back down again. Gideon is a lab like me but with legs he borrowed from a pug. He thinks barking makes him run faster. The rest of us soon join in and that makes the handlers cover their ears. I can only conclude that a human's ear gets cold when dogs bark so they use their hands to warm them up. Marley is the best agility dog in our group and has won lots of ribbons but everyone is awesome.

Running agility makes Tim smile so I do the very best I can. Sometimes a human's eyes become moist when they are happy and that seems to happen to Tim when I win a ribbon. I love to run. I love to climb. I run agility, however, because I love the smell of pride that pours out from Tim whenever we run, win or lose.

Next to Tim is food. I'm not picky. In my life I have found all sorts of tasty morsels in the strangest places. Living with Josh was like being on an all-day treasure hunt. Crumbs just seemed to follow him and I was not far behind. For the record, I can empty a dog bowl faster than a squirrel climbs a tree and come back for more. Sometimes I get treats just for doing what Tim asks. He's much better at speaking "dog" than he used to be. He calls it training but sometimes I am the teacher. As humans go, he catches on fast. I guess I have taught him well. Yes, food is good.

Dog parks are great but sometimes they are crowded and not all the dogs are polite. When I am outside, I love to hike on a trail in the mountains or in the woods. The smells of the forest are intoxicating and I sometimes forget where I am as I try to track them down. I'm not a bloodhound but my nose rarely leads me astray. If it's out there, I'll find it. I especially like to climb because it lets my front leg rest while my back legs get to work for a change. The best climbing places ever are close to where Josh lives now. Tim and I recently explored some trails through mountains so high that they touched the clouds. On this trip I learned that deer are much faster than dogs. Worst of all, they know it and will let you get close before disappearing into the trees. Tim doesn't let me chase deer anymore.

Besides humans, my favorite animals are squirrels and rabbits. Notice there was no mention of cats? I chase them because they want me to. One day I will catch one and will carry it proudly in my mouth and drop it at Tim's feet. He will be so pleased with me. I tried to bring him a frog once. That didn't work out so well.

Sleeping ranks right up there with rawhide bones so I'm not sure which I like better. Now that I'm older, I'll go with sleep. I try not to let Tim see when I'm tired or when the muscles in my leg ache from too much hiking or running. He doesn't know when I need to rest so sometimes I just lay down wherever I can find some shade. I'll sleep half the day when I get home and I sleep when Tim goes to work. I also sleep when Tim turns out the lights. If that sounds like a lot, try hopping around on one leg for a couple of days and see how you feel.

This one makes Tim crazy. I like to pee where other animals have been. It's sort of like signing a guest book and I'm quite certain the next dog will want to know that I was there first. We make a lot of stops on our walks and I can smell the frustration in Tim if I do it too much. By the way, humans like Tim need to understand something. Pooping takes time. Don't rush us.

Tim is my favorite human but Grandma is awesome too. She's the one person who loves Tim more than I do and that's saying something. Josh is my boy too but we don't see him much these days. The PetSmart people are wonderful, too. I like Kathy best. Yes, she gives me enough treats to fill a bathtub but I can smell that she loves dogs. Brian is a mountain as humans go. I've never met one whose head is so close to the sky. Plants need water to grow and so do dogs. I think Brian's mother must have watered him daily when he was a puppy. Brian and his daughter Nesha cared for me when Tim went away for several days. I knew I could count on them to feed me and take me on walks. Dustin kept me from being lonely when he lived with us. An evil car must have hit him once because his foot doesn't work very well. I like him because he walks like me.

But I am for Tim. That is what I do and it brings me great joy. When the day comes for my eyes to close forever, I will greet him on a trail in the mountains and we will forever be hiking together and running agility courses.

I love to be outside when it's cold and the ground is covered with that wet and wonderful white stuff known to you as snow. My idea of fun is burying my nose in a drift and watching it spray in all directions. Tim likes to kick snow in my face then laughs as I snort and bite at the air. I tire more easily in the summer. Tim and I are opposites that way. He likes the heat even when it makes his face wet. As for me, I'm heading for the shade and a bowl of water.

Here's a little known fact about dogs. Our tongues itch. Have you ever tried to scratch your tongue? Fortunately for me, Tim's chin grows these prickly little hairs and it makes the most exquisite scratching post. A human's tongue is much shorter than mine and I wonder what people do when their tongues itch.

All in all, it's a pretty good life. Far too many of my kind spend their days as tie-down dogs. Others run free with no purpose. Still some live with humans who are too busy for them. I wish that could change. If only humans could be dogs for just a day. Through our eyes, the world looks a lot different.

I have cursed thy rod and staff
They no longer comfort me
Love rescue me . . ."

Bono and Bob Dylan. *"Love Rescue Me"*

CHAPTER 25: FOR JOSH

There would be no more agility competitions for two years. I began working both Saturday and Sunday in an attempt to promote more pet training sales. It seemed to be working and I was asked to share the secrets of my success with other stores. My days off were Monday and Friday. No one was offering agility classes on those days.

Word was spreading that I had some clue as to what I was doing. People came into the store to pick my brain about training subjects ranging from cat herding to a fear of a vacuum cleaner. I made it a point to read the various works of Pat Miller, Victoria Stillwell, Ian Dunbar, Suzanne Hetts, and of course, Dr. McConnell. "The Other End of the Leash" should be required reading for anyone who views dogs as more than a snow blower or a yard ornament.

I wanted to share the wonder of Dixie with the world and found a perfect outlet through therapy dog work. Dixie breezed through the testing and was certified in the winter of 2009 with a local organization called "Pets For Life." We were assigned to a local hospital as well as a residential home for children who had been removed from their homes due to abuse and neglect. Dixie was to be a conduit for hope in the lives of the downtrodden.

Patients at the hospital found it difficult to wallow in self-pity when the dog with three legs came to call. Dixie sat quietly as I told her story of courage and triumph. I'd like to think that their recoveries were expedited by our visits. Perhaps the most poignant moment came at the children's residential facility. A little boy who had been silent for most of his two week stay approached us from the corner of the room.

"I have a dog too" he said softly as he stroked Dixie's back.

Dixie thoroughly enjoyed her visits each week and I could think of no more rewarding experience for any pet owner.

PetSmart store managers were sending me their new hires to be molded into dog trainers in what I jokingly referred to as "Tim the Trainer's Boot Camp." My classes were full and the paychecks began to approach what I was making as an early education center director. My professional life was more fulfilling than I thought possible after leaving early education. But there was no Josh.

In fact, he was no longer returning weekly calls or e-mails. Weeks would go by without contact. It was as though he was sinking in desert quicksand and refusing to grab my outreached hand. I was able to track his grades on line and he was still failing nearly every class. At this rate, he would be the only high school senior old enough buy beer for his buddies. Written comments from his teachers whistled a common tune.

"He's a great kid. He just doesn't do anything."

My frustrations began to mount. Before visiting Josh in the spring of 2009, I tried to contact his teachers and academic counselors for suggestions as to how I could help my son only to be told they could share nothing with me without proof of identity. To school teachers and administrators, I was just a voice over the phone. While I respected their desire to protect my son's privacy, there was no way to convince them that I was Josh's father from 1,200 miles away.

His counselor did agree to set up a meeting with Josh's teachers after school on the day that I arrived in Chino Valley. Only two showed up and the counselor was nowhere to be found. Neither teacher was forthcoming and seemed uncomfortable releasing any information about Josh beyond what

I had read on line. It was as though they were not sure what to do with an absent parent who gave a damn.

This was not the only setback during this trip. I received a call from the Board President of Pets For Life. Apparently he had done a Google search of my name for reasons he would not make clear. Upon learning of the charge levied against me, he felt it best that we no longer participate as a therapy dog team. In short, Dixie and I were fired and feelings of worthlessness resurfaced.

Driving through the majestic deserts of the American Southwest and the golden wheat fields of the Great Plains towards Kansas City gives one ample time to think. I pushed the "scan" button on my car radio but repeatedly landed on National Public Radio, the twang of classic country music, or a preacher from the Old Time Gospel Hour professing that the Bible was my salvation.

A lifetime of Christian propaganda provided no clarity. Ultimately, it had led me to a spiritual impasse somewhere in Monument Valley National Park. Feeling strung out from the road, I pulled the truck into a rest area and gazed into the glorious rock formations. Each was a work of art all its own. It occurred to me that perhaps a higher power stirred the primordial goo that set all this in motion but it did not create the events that shaped my life nor would it offer salvation for the struggles I had faced. My Christian education had erroneously led me to believe that the their God had a plan for me and every other "believer." Only "divine intervention" could explain the mix of fate and coincidence that produced all things wonderful.

I wondered if this could this be the same "God" that declined to intervene while thousands were victimized by starvation and political tyranny throughout the world every day. An arbitrary "God" that allowed suffering on a planetary scale while delivering a family home safely from their weekend vacation cottage was not worthy of my devotion. My closest friends Brian, Phil, and Dustin are Christians of the finest kind. So is Mom. Their faith allows them to make sense of the world and provides a source of comfort. I respect that as I do all beliefs. But praying to and believing in a mythical being did not bring me to Dixie or deliver me from the court system, and it was not going to blaze a path to my doorstep for Josh to follow. My son needed me and prayers were not going to help. I was 1,200 miles away and could nothing for him.

Prescott, Arizona had been my home during the happiest years of my life. I had met Yvonne and our relationship, though doomed, was in its infancy. My passion then was softball and I played nearly eighty games a year. We traveled throughout Arizona playing weekend tournaments and evening league games. My career at Big Brothers/Big Sisters was evolving to the point where I would eventually be hired to direct my own agency. I met my spiritual leader, Jerry Burd, and learned about the mountains and a simpler life, void of excessive material wants.

It was time to return to Prescott. Josh needed me and I needed him. My softball team was no more and the community had doubled its population. If Dixie and I were not eligible to volunteer as a therapy dog team, it was clear that I would never work with children again despite being acquitted of the charge. Picking up with Big Brothers/Big Sisters was not an option. Jerry had become disenchanted with the ministry and was now a wine maker in New Mexico. My old softball team was composed of guys half my age. I didn't know anyone in Prescott save Josh and my ex-wife. At least the mountains were still there. And I had Dixie for company.

At least on the surface, Mom was supportive of my decision to leave Kansas City. Down deep, she felt I was setting myself up for yet another disappointment. I understood her concerns and shared them to some degree but getting my son back was not without its risks. The first step was to put in for a transfer at PetSmart. There was a store in Prescott and apparently they were in need of a pet trainer so I was in luck. In May of 2009, I loaded my belongings in the back of a U-Haul truck, and towed my vehicle into Prescott. Dixie rode shotgun and seemed to sense that things were about to change. She loved the desert, and the central Arizona mountains. There were countless trails we had yet to conquer.

We settled into a two bedroom apartment conveniently close to a hiking trail and just minutes from work. Phil was swamped as usual with insurance claims so he was unable to make the drive with me but flew out for the weekend to help unload the truck. Josh joined us and it was like old times. When we lived in Topeka, Josh and I made weekend trips to Kansas City and hung out with "Uncle Phil." This reunion brought back fond memories.

It took about two hours to empty the back of the U-Haul, which left the rest of the day for a hike and a movie. Later I took Josh home and dreamt of the days ahead filled with treks through the mountains, bike rides, movies, and just general "bumming" around.

Phil wanted to hike so we set out the next morning on what I thought was a familiar trail. My sense of direction has never been keen. In fact, I often relied on Dixie's built-in navigation system to direct me when I reached a fork in the trail. If she had been there once, she seemed to always know the way. I have embarrassed myself on more than one occasion when I allowed her good judgment on the trails to be overridden by my own silly pride. In this case, I had last hiked the White Spar trail well before Dixie was born, so naturally I managed to get us hopelessly lost.

Our goal had been to hike the morning away and dine at a local eatery for lunch. As a result of getting lost, that noon meal was delayed until 3 p.m. We were famished but much better off than Dixie. Our water ration exhausted, Dixie began suffering cramps in her front leg and would collapse every twenty yards or so like a car warbling down the road on a hopelessly flat tire. The strain of the hike was evident on her face as her gait turned into one agonizing lurch after another. We stopped repeatedly to let her rest but were driven by hunger to push forward.

Dixie was lame the next day and I felt like the most neglectful dog owner on the planet. We had hiked about 15 miles. For the next three days, my super trooper could barely limp outside to relieve herself. I made an appointment with a local vet who immediately put her on a healthy dose of Rimadyl for a week. She was back to normal in a few days but my guilt lingered much longer.

I was unaccustomed to being the new guy on the block at PetSmart. I had developed a clientele and a reputation as a competent trainer in Overland Park but no one knew me in Prescott and it was difficult to adjust. The other trainer was more established and taught the majority of the classes.

I was regulated to duty as a cashier in between what few classes I was assigned to teach. The store was a morgue during the day which meant I had little to do but stand and make small talk with whomever walked by. I maintained my rank as area trainer but had no hopes of performing that aspect of my job anytime soon. I was told by store manager Travis that I would be teaching more classes if sales improved. Unfortunately, I didn't have much of an impact on the bottom line while tethered to a cash register.

I called Josh every other day or so but was getting no response to my messages. When time permitted, I made the drive to little Chino Valley and knocked on the door but was never able to rouse anyone. A month had passed and I had not seen Josh since the day I moved into my apartment.

Once a social butterfly, I was no longer comfortable meeting people and had been relying on familiar relationships for companionship. Back in Overland Park there were Phil, Brian, Dustin, and Ed to pass time with. Glenda and Angie were in Topeka. But in Prescott there was no one except Dixie. We spent our days hiking, walking the courthouse square downtown, and attending outdoor concerts. Our only friend was the owner of a little downtown dog boutique. The shop sold nothing we could afford but the proprietor was enamored with Dixie. Once again, she refused to allow me to crawl inside the tortoise shell I had been lugging on my back since the trial.

Life at PetSmart had taken a downward turn as well. My hours were being cut gradually and I set out to get a second job. Gainful employment was scarce all over but more so in Arizona than in Kansas. The local Target store wasn't even hiring. I was 49 years old working as an overpaid cashier with nothing but time on my hands.

Thankfully, there was a dog park within walking distance of my apartment. Better still, they had some agility equipment in various stages of disrepair. Each day after work, Dixie and I walked to the park to practice on hurdles and tunnels. But even that ray of sunshine clouded over when one grumpy patron complained about me wearing a treat bag attached to my belt and demanded that I leave. I've never responded well to bullying and the confrontation left me anxious to the point that we only went back to the park if it was empty. The presence of even one person being there with his dog was enough to turn us toward a nearby trail where we disappeared along a dusty path to nowhere.

Bike rides were my other source of solace. Summer's wrath could be felt even in the mountains. Exposed skin can burn within twenty minutes so I chose early morning jaunts into the foothills and quiet suburban streets. Dixie barked in protest as I walked my bike outside the apartment door, knowing full well she would be staying behind. The feel of the morning mountain breeze kissing my face and blowing back the wisps of hair that remained was a rush that I rarely denied myself. I missed my bike rides with Brian. It was late July and still I had not heard from Josh.

"Why am I even here?" I asked Dixie during a midnight walk.

The answer was not forthcoming.

The whole point was to be close to Josh the way a father should and to be his advocate. I was failing miserably on both counts. To make matters worse, I was making considerably less money and the cost of living in Arizona was much higher than expected.

In July I learned of agility classes being taught in the same little town where Josh resided and I enthusiastically registered with what funds I had left. The instructor was knowledgeable but had the disposition of a giraffe with acid reflux.

"What's the matter with you people, can't you get this?" she screamed to the class one evening.

Apparently we had not grasped a concept she awkwardly tried to teach. An eerie silence fell over the class and I opted not to return. My request for a refund of class fees was met with an emphatic "Hell, no!" Through no fault of her own, Dixie was again denied access to a sport she loved.

Once more, depression hitched itself to me like an anchor and there were days that I felt myself sinking to the bottom of the ocean. Once again, Dixie was like a lifeline lowered into the water as I spiraled downward.

Our time on the trails, at the doggie boutique, and walking Prescott's historical courthouse square kept me afloat and reminded me why life on most days was worth living.

By August the well had run dry. My hours at PetsMart had been reduced to thirty a week. The move to Arizona was costly and my legal bills had drained the modest savings I had accumulated over the years. Outside my classroom was a kiosk chock full of information about training classes as well as a box where customers could deposit a slip of paper requesting a free thirty minute behavior consultation. This rarely happened in our store so I took notice when I saw that there was a single piece of paper collecting dust at the bottom on the box.

I retrieved the slip to find that it had nothing to do with pet training. It read "Tim, just kill yourself. Think of the children."

The message was unsigned and left no room for interpretation. It was time to go home and start over once again.

There was no money for a U-Haul. In fact, I wasn't sure if I had enough gas money to make it far as Denver.

"What the hell," I mused. "I always wanted to live in Colorado."

What didn't fit into the back of my Honda was sold. My furniture, bed, and my clothes were on the selling block. I took whatever I could get and came away with $300 for the trip to Overland Park.

Two days before I departed vowing never to return, I left a rather sarcastic message with Josh explaining why I was leaving and that I wanted to see him again. An all too cruel irony awaited me in the form of a reply on my cell. It was Josh, sounding like we had seen one another only last week. He wanted to hike a trail we had conquered before at the base of Granite Mountain.

I have had lower back problems for years and had managed to tweak it while moving furniture so I was in no condition to hike. Josh was indifferent to my plight and I forged ahead as though I were sporting a body cast.

Uneven portions of the trail were particularly painful and of course Josh wanted to climb rocks and bushwhack with little regard for the natural beauty he was disturbing. I was in no mood to argue so hobbled along as best I could thinking I had a 1,200 mile car ride to rehabilitate my aching back. Five year old Dixie, who hiked like she had the hooves of a bighorn sheep, forged ahead while looking back periodically to see if we plodding humans were keeping pace.

Naturally I asked Josh why my calls had not been returned. Apparently he had received some but not all of them and was surprised to learn that I had been calling so frequently. Still, he seemed indifferent and I sensed he had called out of some misguided sense of obligation. His only reply was that he had been busy. It was summer. He had no job and was not in school. Just what did the kid do all day?

We visited a local used bookstore. Thankfully, Josh's love of reading carried over from his days with me but I wasn't quite sure if he actually finished the books I bought him or that he retrieved from the library. The Harry Potter series was his favorite and the movies had an almost cult-like appeal to him. I discovered, however, that he had developed an interest in some darker imagery. Perhaps his reality had become so unpleasant that he needed to immerse himself in a fantasy world of dungeons, dragons, and gothic themes. His description of the characters sometimes intruded on real time and I must admit to catching myself totally disinterested in what he was saying. I was no closer to him now than I was when I arrived. The move to Arizona was an utter and complete failure. In fact, I could feel him slipping from my grasp.

My last day in Prescott was spent with Dixie, just as every other day had been since I landed in this idyllic little town. I loved the mountains, as did Dixie, and was saddened by the reality that we may not see them again for a while.

Dixie has a remarkable zest for life on most days but it reached new heights when hiking a trail—any trail—anywhere (yes, even the Kansas City metro has hiking trails). Don't tell the park rangers but she nearly always hikes off leash, darting off the well-worn path to investigate some intriguing scent with her extraordinary olfactory system before hustling back to check in with me. The first mile of the hike is comical, as she more resembles a drunken pinball bouncing from one side of the trail to the other in search of that which only she knows.

We hiked familiar places and hit the dog park (it was vacant, of course). I then loaded the car for the journey home. This time there would be no looking back.

"Second star to the left . . . straight ahead till morning."

*"It's been awhile
Since I could hold my head up high
And it's been awhile
Since I could stand on my own two feet again…"*

Staind, *"It's Been Awhile"*

CHAPTER 26: WHO SAYS YOU CAN'T COME HOME?

PetSmart has intranet technology that enables 1,200 plus stores to communicate with one another and with the corporate office in Phoenix. Before leaving Prescott, I sent out an e-mail to stores in the Kansas City area announcing that I was unceremoniously returning and needed a job. Apparently this type of shameless self-promotion didn't sit well with the district manager so responses were guarded at best. One came from Kathy, my former manager in Overland Park who had since been assigned to another store. She had a part time position and suggested that I might contact other stores to see if I could split my time until she had something more permanent. Naturally she asked about Dixie. I accepted her offer to work part time.

The second response I received was from Don Edwards who managed the smallest store in the district at a mall on the Missouri side of the city. He too had only part time hours so I signed on with that store, just thankful to have a job upon my return.

I had stayed in touch via e-mail with best friends Brian, Dustin, and Ed. E-mail was my favorite form of correspondence though I was curious about this thing called Facebook. While social networking was the cornerstone of pop culture, it was new to my world. I'm a bit of a relic when it comes to technology. Ironically, I never communicated via e-mail or Facebook with my best friend Phil. We talked on the phone at least weekly. It had always been that way and we saw no reason to break with tradition.

Dustin was certain he could not afford rental property in affluent Johnson County, Kansas so he remained at home with his parents and four younger siblings. I suggested we become roommates and he quickly jumped on board. His dad was a bit dubious as to why a 49 year old man would want to live with a kid young enough to be his son.

It just so happened that Dustin and I got along famously in our two bedroom apartment with a few sticks of furniture and cable TV. Our PetSmart shifts were opposite one another so we each enjoyed hours of uninterrupted privacy which I found was conducive to peaceful coexistence. That having been said, we spent a fair amount of our off hours together until a girlfriend became a fiancée. Dustin loved dogs and cared for Dixie during my PetSmart shifts so it was the best of times for a dog who was never thrilled at the prospect of being left alone.

Soon after my return, Don was able to create a full time training position at the little store in Missouri and it became my permanent assignment. This was my fourth PetSmart store and I was determined to make it my final stop. A loyal clientele would bring steady sales commissions but I needed to be housed in one location for at least a year to establish a referral network. I thoroughly enjoyed working for Don. His laid back style and self-deprecating humor were the perfect recipe for my recovery from yet another setback.

The former trainer told me that this little store was like a cell phone dead zone in terms of sales. I needed a challenge like this to revive the passion for pet training squelched by the Arizona experience. The store was several thousand dollars short of its sales plan for pet training when I arrived. We finished the fiscal year just $200 under the plan. Classes were filling, sales improved, and pet training became a priority for the management team. I teased district manager Jamie that our tiny store was the proverbial "little engine that could."

The joys of professional success, however, rarely followed me home. Off hours watching mindless television programming was turning my brain to oatmeal. Two shows were the exception. There was ABC's quirky "Boston Legal" and "24," my favorite all-time drama series. The Jack Bauer character was flawed and fragile much like myself and I connected with that aspect of his personality. Jack, the counter-terrorism operative, and me, the pacifist were strange bedfellows. Yet I found the Monday night episodes riveting and howled in frustration as the final seconds of the episode ticked away, knowing I would have to wait six agonizing days to learn our country's fate against the evil forces of terrorism.

I needed to do something to rekindle the professional fires so I enrolled at Animal Behavior College in search of dog training certification. On-line schooling was a new concept to me and I wondered if I was up to the task of completing this program without ever setting foot on the Northridge, California campus.

Financial aid was available but at a higher interest rate than my credit card so I begrudgingly bit the bullet and plunked nearly three grand down on my Visa. PetSmart benefits included a $1,200 reimbursement for continuing education and I intended to make full use of that perk. Sadly, PetSmart amended its policy of supporting professional certifications in favor of four year degree programs so I was ultimately stuck with the tab.

There would be four requirements for earning this certification. First would be the reading of two texts, followed by a test over each section. Secondly, I would need to complete 10 volunteer hours training dogs at a local shelter. Next was the internship with a local trainer. Finally, I would need to pass a final exam including an essay portion. I could work at my own pace but was expected to complete the program in 18 months.

Improving my pet training credentials meant less time for Dixie. Patiently she would wait for the books to close and then perk her ears in anticipation for a study break, which usually took the form of some outdoor recreation. The highlight of her week came when she accompanied me to work as a demonstration dog for the new hires I was training. Don and PetSmart had parted ways and my former manager Kathy was assigned to the store. Kathy loved Dixie and filled her belly with Bil-Jac training treats whenever she came into the store. I joked to other associates that Kathy was the "grandmother from Hell" because she never made Dixie work for her food the way that I did.

To this day, Dixie makes a beeline for Kathy's office the moment the automatic door slides open. The disappointment in her eyes is heartbreaking when she peers into the office window to find Kathy's chair occupied by another manager. Kathy's arrival at the Ward Parkway PetSmart certainly met with Dixie's approval.

We continued our morning jogs. I wasn't training for a marathon so I limited our runs to three miles on the average of three times a week. We also took training walks where she would perform a different trick at each street corner. I was working both Saturday and Sunday now as well as four evenings a week so taking another agility class was not an option. No one taught on Friday, Saturday, or Sunday nights and that was all I had available. It saddened me to think her agility career had come to a screeching halt after just one competition. Though Dixie was five years old now and not getting any younger, she had certainly not received any invitations from the AARP. Surely there was something I could do for my dear friend to enrich her life as well as mine.

How about acting?

"Oh yes they call him the Streak
Fastest thing on two feet
He's just as proud as he can be
Of his anatomy . . ."

Ray Stevens, "The Streak"

CHAPTER 27: LIGHTS, CAMERA . . . REALLY?

I should have known better and just trusted my instincts. This was a bad idea from the beginning but the thrill of Dixie appearing in a feature length motion picture caused me to take temporary leave of my senses.

It all began with an e-mail I received from a friend of a friend. Apparently a local production company was putting out a casting call for—get this—dogs with three legs. A representative from Hallmark Cards (based right here in Kansas City) once contacted me about having Dixie model for them and I agreed as long as the card didn't poke fun at her condition. They never called back. I was therefore suspicious of the production company's motives though intrigued enough to call the talent wrangler for this project. The movie was titled "Kick Me" and was scheduled for a holiday release.

The dogs were needed for a scene to be shot in a vacant shopping mall. An actor playing the role of the hero was to run through the mall with the dogs in hot pursuit. Somehow that presence of three legged dogs would add a splash of humor to what the crew described as an action/comedy. There was also to be a scene where the dogs warm up to the villain who enters the mall in search of our winded hero.

"Ah, I get it," I said, though I really didn't. "Chase the good guy, love on the bad guy. Funny stuff. Count us in."

All the while I contemplated the hallucinogen of choice when this scene was conceived.

We were asked to arrive at the mall by 6 p.m. but were told the scene would not be shot until nine due to some technical delay. It was a warm summer evening and so we headed for the comfort of a climate controlled mall only to find that the air conditioning had not been turned on. Apparently that minor detail wasn't negotiated into the permit to use the facility. Dixie and I, along with five other "tripawds" and their increasingly skeptical owners, huddled in the limited shade available in a mall parking lot.

Shortly before nine, the director gathered us together to confess that one minor detail was omitted from his description of the mall scene. The male actor would be wearing nothing more than an athletic supporter. We stood stunned for a moment while the director explained that partial nudity was a metaphor for a world that had literally taken the shirt right off the character's back. Apparently it took a lot more than that.

To my amazement, no one backed out. In fact, we followed the director like sheep right into the stuffy mall where we met a chiseled Hispanic man wearing a bath robe. I assumed he was the object of the dog's pursuit. As a trainer, I wondered how the crew planned to entice these dogs to chase a naked man through the mall. I soon discovered that there was no plan in place. The director simply expected to shout "action" and the chase would be on.

"Cut!" he bellowed, as the dogs sniffed the floor while the cheeky actor sprinted through the mall.

After multiple takes, it was time for some intervention. I reluctantly introduced myself to the director hoping this would not result in my name appearing in the movie credits as the three legged dog trainer. Imagine some Hollywood producer putting out a nationwide search for the dog trainer with three legs. I gave him several options for engaging the dogs in a chase. Ultimately, the most successful ploy involved having production assistants hold the dogs, as all but Dixie were clueless as to the "wait" command. Meanwhile, the owners would stand behind the camera panning in reverse and frantically call their dogs. It took over an hour but we got the shot.

Next was a scene that called for the dogs to listen intently to an actor telling a grisly story of a woman's fingers being chewed off and eventually sewn back on. Of course the dogs had no interest in the dialogue and wandered off set. The director turned to me and I suggested he tighten the shot and keep the dog's attention by having an actor covertly dispense treats from his hand. For the most part, this seemed to work so it was on to the final scene. All the while I desperately racked my brain for an alias in case he actually asked for my name. Fortunately, he did not and my identity remained a mystery to the production crew.

We were all hot, tired and a little cranky at this point. I had worked my PetSmart shift earlier in the day and it was well past midnight. We were introduced to a young man who was going to portray a cadaver. It was to appear as though the dogs were chowing down on the corpse. In preparation, the crew went about meticulously smearing the kid with Alpo canned dog food. A warning light went off in the control room of my trainer brain. A pack of unfamiliar dogs in close proximity lapping canned by-products from a human body spelled disaster. I expressed my concerns to the director who had clearly never heard of food aggression in dogs then politely withdrew Dixie from the shoot and headed for the parking lot.

In the distance I heard snarling and the gnashing of teeth followed closely by the shrill screams of a young actor who probably wished he had a stunt double. I assumed my concerns were well founded. It was 2 a.m. and time for us to go. Be sure to pick up a copy of "Kick Me" at a flea market or Dollar General near you.

Dixie's movie career was officially on hold. The task of keeping her mentally and emotionally stimulated was still a priority.

Enter Oreo.

"If you got troubles
I got them too
There isn't anything
I wouldn't do for you..."

Randy Newman, "You've Got a Friend in Me"

CHAPTER 28: THE GIFT

PetSmart donates valuable retail space to reputable rescue groups on the weekends and partners with them to promote pet adoption. It's a worthy endeavor given that an estimated four million companion animals are euthanized each year simply because we cannot find suitable homes for them. Behavior problems are the primary reason dogs are relinquished to shelters. Positive pet training offers proven strategies for reducing unwanted behaviors such as soiling, destructive chewing, barking, digging, poor leash skills, jumping on great-grandma (I do encourage this behavior, however, with in-laws!), puppy biting, leash reactivity, etc. I find great fulfillment knowing I am doing my part to end this senseless genocide in my little corner of the world.

The group chosen as an adoption partner at the Ward Parkway PetSmart store is the Heart of America Humane Society (HAHS). Don't bother looking up their street address. HAHS is a network of foster homes providing temporary care to dogs and cats who are about to walk the green mile at two local "kill" shelters. By definition, these facilities must euthanize animals due to pet overpopulation. Others must perish to make room for new arrivals.

Many HAHS volunteers sought my advice over the years in dealing with their foster pets. I also allowed them to use my classroom for "meet and greets" on Saturdays between scheduled classes. A friendly relationship had been forged.

In September of 2009, I watched a foster parent trying to coax a black and white mixed breed dog into the store. The squatty little dog hunkered down in the parking lot and looked something like a spotted speed bump. Sensing the volunteer's frustration, I offered my assistance and eased the dog into the store with a treat called Pupperoni® which we trainers affectionately call "puppy crack."

Sure enough, the dog eventually made it to the door but pancaked to the floor upon entering the store. Her eyes darted about as panic set in. Her pupils were dilated in broad daylight. She trembled and her tail was tucked so that it was barely visible. The little girl was frightened and only the den-like environment of a steel kennel seemed to set her at ease. With two black spots over her eyes separated by a white strip of fur along her forehead and across the bridge of her nose, the logical name given to her by the shelter was "Oreo."

She was unlike any dog I had ever met. Her right earflap nearly always stood at attention while the left one was flaccid. She was as wide as she was tall, looking like a dwarfed Dalmatian. The eyes were engaging, gentle, unassuming, yet vulnerable. Each Saturday, I took a few minutes between teaching classes to work on basic commands. She would make a great companion for someone if I could help her interact more confidently with her environment. We took a quick liking to one another and a bond began to grow with each passing week.

Oreo's foster parent explained that she had been left in an outdoor kennel most of her life and was abandoned when it was discovered that she was pregnant. Her swollen teats indicated that she had not been apart from her puppies very long. We guessed that Oreo was around 5 years of age. Her kennel card read "pit mix" which severely limited the prospects for adoption on the Kansas side of the state line. Most of Johnson County had bought into mindless breed ordinances so Kansans seeking a new pet bypassed Oreo time and again. Her puppies found homes right away but no one wanted mama dog.

Our Saturday sessions continued and she would stare longingly at me as I returned her to her kennel. I naively promised myself that I would not become emotionally attached to my canine students but there was no erasing the image of that funny little critter from my mind. It would take a very special dog to co-exist with diva Dixie. Besides, I lived in Johnson County. There was no way a "pit mix" could be licensed no matter how often I threw myself on the mercy of the animal control officers.

The more time I spent with Oreo, the more strongly I felt that she had been mislabeled by overworked and underpaid shelter staff so I came up with a plan. First, I asked foster parent Julie to meet me at the animal control office in Leawood, Kansas where I had arranged for an officer to venture a guess as to her breed. The response: "Pointer mix."

A week later Julie and I brought Oreo to another jurisdiction and the verdict was the same. Oreo was a pointer mix and did not display enough of the AKC breed standards to be classified as a pit or any of the other "aggressive" breeds listed on the ordinance. In November, with roommate Dustin's blessing, Oreo came home to meet Dixie for the first time. If it didn't work out, I could return Oreo to the foster parent with no questions asked.

Frankly, I didn't know what would happen. To live harmoniously with Dixie, Oreo would have to be the queen of submission, deferring to Dixie on all things. Any challenges over resources would be met with an immediate rebuke. I took custody of Oreo at the Julie's office. She clearly recognized me and cheerfully hopped in the back of my Honda Element for the ride home to meet her Highness. Dixie greeted Oreo without so much as a grunt and the two exchanged crotch sniffs. Oreo wandered the apartment and settled in for a nap. Dixie went about her business. So far, so good.

There were two altercations over food. Dixie moved to stake her claim but it was Oreo, not Dixie that took exception with a snarl. Dixie quickly backed away and the line had been drawn in the sand. In all other matters it was Oreo giving way to Dixie and the social dynamics of our family had been established within a few days. Oreo was here to stay and I was pleased that Dixie would have a companion to fill the empty hours while I waged an ongoing battle with the demons that imprisoned my soul.

Oreo was still afraid of her own shadow but was born to walk on a leash and mastered "heel" in half the time it took Dixie. I purchased a "coupler" that enabled me to walk both dogs with a single leash. This clever little device saved time not to mention wear and tear on my 50 year old legs. Oreo took the inside. Dixie preferred the outside and both walked quite politely on my left. Eventually, I removed the lead and the dogs learned to walk bound only by the coupler.

Dixie and I taught Oreo to sit at intersections or any other time we came to a stop. She picked up sit/stay quickly but couldn't wrap her head around "down" so some shaping was in order. A few hot dogs later, Oreo's belly was on the floor. The "stay" part of that cue meant adding chicken to the treat menu.

Part of my internship with Animal Behavior College involved actually taking a class with my dog. I chose Oreo, as we had never actually enrolled in a training class. The class took place at a facility in Blue Springs, MO with the appropriate acronym of DOG (Dog Obedience Group.) Basic skills were taught and Oreo knew most of them from our work at home. She passed with ease. Still, it was a huge accomplishment for this timid little dog. Oreo has proven to be the perfect blend of temperament, size, and intelligence. Fortunate am I to have such a presence in my life.

While Dixie loved people regardless of size, gender, ethnicity, or special abilities, Oreo was a bit more cautious with strangers and was downright terrified of children. Conversely, Oreo was rarely reactive around other dogs, choosing to tuck her tail and lower her hindquarters in a submissive gesture anytime another dog approached. She did not enjoy roughhousing and would tooth snap and cry out at any dog that didn't recognize the meaning of her body tuck. Dixie was a bit of a bully when it came to playing with Oreo. She's really quite the furry hypocrite, taking great offense to rambunctious play with strange dogs while tugging poor Oreo around by her collar.

Oreo was no dunce and discovered quickly that she could out run and out maneuver Dixie on any given day. Many the time I laughed out loud as Oreo ran figure eights around Dixie daring her to chase. The wise old girl simply sat in a predatory crouch like a lioness stalking an otherwise oblivious wildebeest and waited patiently until her quarry was in range. Dixie would lunge as Oreo blew past and the chase was on. From a distance it must have seemed like the girls were engaged in mortal combat, as both growled as they ran, with Dixie barking in frustration when Oreo pulled away.

Some sight gags are hilarious no matter how time they are seen. For me, this played out whenever Oreo would playfully nip at Dixie in hopes of baiting her into a game of "catch me if you can." If Dixie didn't immediately give chase, Oreo would come in low and yank Dixie's only front leg, sending her nemesis toppling downward like a house of cards. The expression on Dixie's face seemed to be saying *"game on, sister!"*

While Dixie loved to hike, Oreo relished in the freedom of a dog park. Rarely have I seen an adult dog so joyful as Oreo while in a dead sprint. It was as if her body was releasing captive endorphins by the truckloads. No doubt this was a "high" she had never experienced from her days of dog run captivity. No matter what park we visited, Oreo always headed for the woods to embrace the multitude of smells never available to her before. Dixie, my ever present companion, chose to walk beside me and only occasionally wandered off to see what Oreo was investigating.

Both dogs loved anything small and furry that dared move across their path. Although "leave it" worked most of the time, there were times I felt as though I were reigning in a moose if a squirrel ventured too close. Oreo manages to tree squirrels on a regular basis and then barks frantically as if begging the varmint to come down and play. Dixie was once like Oreo but now chases for only a few yards before breaking off the pursuit. As she matured, Dixie has adapted to her condition by conserving energy and thus increasing her stamina.

One thing is for certain. Dixie always gets her rodent when in that blissful part of sleep known as Dreamland. Many nights I toiled at this book only to be interrupted by a yip followed by convulsions that could easily be mistaken for a grand mal seizure. The eyelids flutter as though suddenly connected to a defibrillator. Her lips curl, revealing fangs in stand-down mode; three legs spasm and twitch as she moves in for the kill. I chuckle and the sound of my voice awakens her as though I had a direct line to her soul. She is not fully alert and I wonder at what point she disconnects from the dream and re-enters this dimension.

How vivid is the imagery in a dog's dream? How long do they retain the dream? Do dogs have nightmares? Do they dream only in the here and now? Are the dreams filled with images of the past or glimpses of the future? Gosh, I wish I could be a dog for a day with the option of staying if I decide their existence is more pure and without the emotional complications of this one. I'm just not sure I can ever get past replacing handshakes and hugs with the sniffing posteriors and genitalia as a form of greeting another of my species.

Oreo dreams too. Ironically, hers are more vocal, though she rarely barks when awake. She twitches just like Dixie but her vocalizations seem to embrace some sort of doggie rapture. Frankly, I don't want to go there and am grateful that Oreo does not provide me with more information than I need.

INSIGHTS: LOOK WHAT FOLLOWED YOU HOME!

Tim often leaves in the morning for a short time. When he returns, he smells like salt. It's the same after we jog. Salt tastes good on my tongue so I'm always looking for a good place to lick. I must admit that it is getting harder to keep pace when we run, especially when it's hot. People don't run very often and when they do it's not much faster than a walk. Dogs run because they want to get somewhere faster. Humans don't appear to have anywhere to go but run anyway.

On this day, Tim left in the morning but I could smell no salt on his skin when he returned. Suddenly I looked up and there was another dog in our home. There were occasional visits from people but never a dog so I stood frozen for a moment. The dog was smaller than I am and a little pudgy. I picked up the faint smell of milk underneath and wondered if she was my mother. She lowered her body and allowed me sniff and I knew right away that she was not my mother. In fact, she was younger and quite overwhelmed by everything around her. Tim called her "Oreo." The name sounded funny coming out of his mouth.

I am frightened by some things. Let's start with the noise made by storms. Sometimes the entire house shakes right after a flash of light in the darkened sky. Pressing up against Tim helps and he often sits with me on the floor until the storm passes. Balloons carrying people that fly over our house are no picnic either.

The worst is a dog that gets too close to my face or wants to play rough. I have learned that curling my lip and snarling at them keeps me safe but I did not feel threatened by Oreo. Actually, she seemed more afraid of me. This was the way I wanted it if she was going to stay with us. Lest we forget, I was here first.

Oreo needed the occasional reminder that the food in my bowl belonged to me as did any chew toy left on the floor. After that, she never challenged me for the things I value and we became close just like puppies with the same mother. Oreo liked to sleep close to Tim. I allowed this because there was more room at the foot of the bed anyway. We invented wonderful games of chase at the dog park that we still play to this day. Oreo is the fastest dog I've ever met. I'll never catch her in a sprint so I have learned to hunch down in the grass and leap at her as she passes. Sometimes I get a mouthful of her neck as she blazes by and it causes her to stumble. That makes my day.

Oreo is my sleeping companion when Tim is away. Sometimes we wrestle on the floor until he comes home then push each other aside to be the first in line for an ear scratch. She lets me go first. I guess she's a keeper.

> *"Ain't three things in this world that's worth a solitary dime*
> *But old dogs and children and watermelon wine*
> *Old dogs care about you even when you make mistakes*
> *God bless little children while they're still too young to hate . . ."*
>
> Tom T. Hall, "Old Dogs, Children and Watermelon Wine"

CHAPTER 29: DROPPING IN AND OUT

Once in a great while I would call Arizona and Josh would answer the phone. He was always polite though not forthcoming about his life in terms of school, friends, or a desire to see me. In the spring of 2010, he announced the he would be coming to Kansas with his mother in July to take in a country music festival that Yvonne had frequented over the years. He was uncertain about the concert date so I checked on line and requested the time off from work.

Stunned was an understatement when Mom's number appeared on my cell one June afternoon while I was on my way to work. Apparently Josh called Grandma to ask if he could stay a few days just minutes before landing on her doorstep. Yvonne did little more than pull out of the driveway and wave. Mom handled it like a professional concierge which I appreciated because she is not one for surprises. I was clearly dumbfounded when Josh came on the line as I sped down Interstate 435.

Why had Yvonne not been more considerate of my mother and of my time? I had already put in for vacation in July. Pet trainers have to request time off well in advance so as not to create a scheduling glitch with classes. It was doubtful that I could get any time off for this visit given the lack of notice.

Store manager Kathy had been aware of my relationship with Josh and granted me a discretionary day later in the week. It was Monday and

Josh was due to leave Friday. I taught the scheduled classes that evening. Admittedly my heart wasn't in it. After dismissing the last class, I rushed home, grabbed the dogs and drove like Jeff Gordon towards Topeka. It was nearly 11 p.m. when I arrived but Josh had waited up. I had not eaten dinner so Mom prepared a couple of burgers while we talked. Josh again conversed as though he had seen me the day before. We talked until well past midnight and I retired to the spare bedroom while Josh crashed on the couch.

I was up with the morning light but Josh slept until well past 10. Two days on the road through two time changes will do that so I resisted the temptation to rouse him in some mischievous way as I once did when I was a full time dad. Squirt guns were my personal favorite. We had little more than two hours together before I had to make the drive back to Kansas City and report to the Ward Parkway PetsMart store. Dixie and Oreo stayed in Topeka with Josh and his grandmother.

Josh was asleep when I arrived in Topeka Tuesday evening. I was strung out from all the driving so went straight to bed. He again slept until 10 the following morning and I didn't have the heart to wake him. We did talk about a trip to his favorite amusement park in Kansas City on the day that Kathy had graciously given me to spend with him. A Thursday of unadulterated fun was just the prescription for us both. I felt an adrenalin rush as I returned to Kansas City for my Wednesday shift.

Mom agreed to "dog-sit" Dixie and Oreo so I could get a good night's sleep in my own bed. I returned to Topeka early Thursday morning and Mom met me with a solemn expression at the door.

"He's gone," she said. "Yvonne showed up and hour ago and said they were heading home."

Josh's sudden departure took me back to that dark little room in my mind where only the most desperate thoughts are stored. All I could think of was the goodbye we shared the day before as I prepared to return to Kansas City. It was more than just a man hug. It was an embrace and a moment that I cling to even today, for it would be the last time I would see my son.

July of 2010 almost made me feel human again. I turned the big 5-0 which was more of a milestone than a concession. My sister Amy returned to Kansas for the first time in years for her high school reunion with ten year old son Dylan in tow. I had not seen Dylan since he was five and we immediately hit it off.

A few days later, a good friend from Pennsylvania came to visit with her four children and we spent a day at the amusement park. Although I had known Delcie since she was a 9 year old client with Big Brothers/Big Sisters, I had not met her children. She had just separated from her husband and was on a pilgrimage home to Manhattan, Kansas to visit family and friends. This was to be the first real contact with children since the trial and apparently some of the genie's magic was still left in the bottle. The kids, Arylyn, Lydia, Layne, and Bella, were delightful and treated me like a long lost uncle. For a couple of days, I was the Pied Piper again and the tune I played was a familiar one. It felt good to be the "kid guy" again. I can't remember the last time I felt the sheer exuberance of play beyond what I do with the dogs.

"I can't for the life of me
Remember a sadder day
I know they say let it be
But it just don't work out that way..."

Paul Simon, "Mother and Child Reunion"

CHAPTER 30: NOT AGAIN . . .

Occasionally you read about some religious wing nut predicting the apocalypse right down to the last hour. Fortune tellers claim to have insight into the future by shuffling Tarot cards. More often than not these self-proclaimed prophets are as reliable as a rubber crutch. One thing is for certain, however. I will die on the Labor Day weekend, 2000 whatever. The cards are hardly stacked in my favor. To begin with, my marriage ended rather abruptly on one of those fateful three days. Ten years later, I spent part of the Labor Day weekend in jail for a crime I did not commit.

Just days before the Labor Day weekend 2010, I received an e-mail from Arizona about an abuse allegation made by someone near and dear to me. Could things get any worse?

For three hours I sat and stared right through my computer monitor while the life energy drained from by body. Another accusation. Another bold faced lie! And not from an acquaintance. Rather, the accusation came from someone I loved and cherished. How could this be happening? Dixie and Oreo slept peacefully by side but even their presence was no remedy for the venom that was seeping back into my veins.

Dustin came home from an early morning shift and I showed the message to him. His lips pressed together as he read the text and put a compassionate hand on my shoulder.

"I'm really sorry, bud."

Dustin was 23. I'm not sure what I would have said to a friend at that moment when I was his age so I acknowledged his effort with a solemn nod. I needed to talk with someone who had a bit more mileage on the life odometer so drove to Phil's and pulled up the message on his computer. He was furious and we talked for several minutes before I left to hike with the dogs. I needed time to think this through.

My birth family lives in British Columbia and I have remained closest to younger sister Sherri and family. She urged me to open a Facebook account so I could keep up with the Canadian contingent and I reluctantly put a profile together. Admittedly, I enjoyed keeping up with my sister's two children though I hated getting those stupid Farmville updates. When I got home from a hike, two individuals had posted on my wall. One stated that she was going to "friend" all my contacts and tell them what I monster I was. Another said he was "coming to get me" and that I was a "sick mother f . . . ker."

Though a million thoughts were dancing in my head, one message resonated clearly. I was not going to put my family and friends through another investigation and legal ordeal. Mom wouldn't survive another round of this insanity. Flight had taken precedence over fight this time. It was time to go underground. They say that art imitates life. I had become the Jack Bauer character from the "24" television series who so often went into hiding to protect the ones he loved.

I terminated the Facebook and my Yahoo e-mail accounts. My phone number changed that day. And I told Kathy to find a new trainer. For a time, no one would know where I was going. That included Mom, Phil, Brian, and Dustin. They weren't going through them to get to me. If asked, they could honestly reply *"I don't know where he is."*

I researched three possible destinations. First was St. Louis where my dear high school friend Kathy and her husband Thad lived. I had spent Labor Day weekend 2009 with them (I have not been in town on a Labor Day weekend since I was acquitted). They knew about the second accusation and said I could stay indefinitely. There were several PetsMart stores in the area. Surely one of them was hiring.

Option two was to stay with Delcie and the kids outside of Pittsburg, PA. I had asked Kathy for a two week leave of absence but was only granted a week. There was no time to make the drive from St. Louis to Pittsburgh and still remain on the payroll at PetsMart. That was a bridge I could not afford to burn.

Option three was Cedar Rapids, Iowa. I had attended a conference there in 1982 and found the city to be friendly and slow paced. It would be easy to blend into either St. Louis or Cedar Rapids and live out the rest of my life in relative obscurity. I reasoned that if I left Kansas City with no forwarding address, I could keep friends and family from being harassed by whoever might be looking for me. Eventually the storm clouds would clear and I would surface.

I took Dustin to lunch and explained my rationale. There was but one more month left in our lease and he would need to clean up the place and forward my half of the security deposit. We were not going to renew the lease anyway. I gave him my furniture and anything that would not fit in the car. Reluctantly, I relinquished my bike to Brian during the last of our Sunday night bull sessions at Starbucks. He accepted the gift with a frown and expressed concern for my well-being.

Poor Oreo. There was room for only one dog on this journey and Dixie was there first. What an excruciating quandary. No pet owner should have to make that choice. I had taken a young trainer named Sarah through my academy who showed great promise. We struck up a friendship and she adored Oreo. Sarah commented one day that she would take Oreo off my hands in a heartbeat if I ever got tired of her. I assured her that would never happen and I was partially right. By no means had I grown tired of Oreo. I loved her. It came down to an issue of space and expense.

I reluctantly explained my plight to Sarah and she agreed to take Oreo. She owned a rambunctious young German Shepherd Dog that had shown some reactivity to other dogs and I was concerned for Oreo's safety.

We met at a park near her home. Her dog bounded out the car and immediately pounced on a terrified Oreo who coiled into a submissive roll. She whimpered. She cried out and my heart broke. Not only was I abandoning her but I was certain I had placed her very welfare in jeopardy. There were no other options. I handed the leash to Sarah and choked back tears all the way to Topeka. It was time to bid Mom farewell, not knowing if or when I would see her again. Five hours later, we were in St. Louis. I was anything but jovial when I arrived. An ominous cloud had followed me east on I-70 and once again cast a shadow over my soul.

As always, Kathy and Thad were gracious hosts and all but turned over the second floor of their home to Dixie and me. Kathy is a dog lover from way back. Luke and Lily, two Chihuahua mixes she rescued years ago, loved Dixie and she adored them. Chad printed off directions to the various PetsMart stores from Map Quest and I was off in search of a job with a heavy heart. I was not sure I could muster the strength to start over again, much less impress anyone in a job interview.

To my surprise, no one was hiring a trainer. One store manager said he could probably "fit me in" but that I would be assigned to the cash register until enough classes were sold to justify my entry into the classroom. It sounded like Arizona all over again. My certification with Animal Behavior College was nearly completed. In a month or less I would be an Animal Behavior College Certified Dog Trainer. Settling for anything less was not an option. The store in Cedar Rapids had a position open for an area trainer. I hugged my dear friends and thanked them for their hospitality, then set sail for Cedar Rapids.

Dixie and I arrived mid-day and relaxed over a picnic lunch. After a brisk walk through a city park, we drove a short distance to the PetSmart store. Kathy had programmed Dixie to seek out the manager's office for treats so she was in search mode the moment we passed through the sliding door. The only time Dixie pulls on the leash is when we approach the store manager's office at any PetSmart. I had hoped Dixie would be the personification of docility. An unruly dog might spell my doom as a new hire. Not so much. We were greeted warmly by the operations manager who ignored my spastic dog and gave us a quick tour.

The associates were curious about Dixie. I told her story to a captive audience for the umpteenth time. The crowd dispersed and I began scanning the local apartment guide for a place to live. I visited a couple of communities and found one to my liking. The following day, I dropped off the application and initial fee before heading south to Kansas City to gather the rest of my belongings and start a new life in Cedar Rapids.

The plan was formulated on the drive home. I would request an immediate transfer and begin the process of advising my students while not revealing my destination to anyone until I was certain that the investigative trail had grown cold. So far, there had been no inquiries from local law enforcement as to my whereabouts but I was taking no chances. I feared an arrest would again be front page news only this time in a major market. The scrutiny that my friends and Mom would endure would be suffocating. If necessary, I would invoke my passport and flee to Canada. I hoped it would not come to that and I could one day forward my Cedar Rapids address to Mom and friends. Maybe I could even go home.

Oreo was my little "cookie dog" and I missed her dearly. The first order of business was to swing by Topeka and pick Oreo up before Sarah's manic German Shepherd Dog could torment her further. The reunion with Oreo only served to solidify the guilt I felt for leaving her behind in the first place. Her entire body quivered in a euphoric spasm. Greeting her was like trying to capture lightning in a bottle. She even peed and I had never seen that before. Dixie and Oreo exchanged licks across the jowls and a crotch sniff. My family was reunited again.

Poet Robert Burns once said, "The best laid plans of mice and men often go awry." I returned to the Ward Parkway PetSmart store to teach my Saturday classes with a written request for transfer in one hand and a rehearsed statement about my departure in the other. What I had not anticipated was the reaction of my students.

I was but a pet trainer, albeit a decent one, and assumed my impact on the lives of my students was minimal in the grand scheme of things. Yet my carefully crafted announcement was met with genuine surprise and, in some cases, an all-out panic.

"What am I going to do about my dog if you leave?" was a question that confronted me on more than one occasion.

There were many competent trainers out there, I countered, and I offered to refer them to those I respected. But for some crazy reason, they wanted me. Suddenly I felt I was abandoning the people that apparently depended on me more than I imagined. I kept the transfer request pinned to my clipboard and left the store at the end of my shift perplexed as to my next move. It would not come to me until the wee hours of the following morning.

It was time for a "Dixie walk." Though Oreo accompanied us now, this was a route that amped Dixie up more than a butcher bone. The suburban hike took us from the apartment I once shared with Dustin several blocks south, then west across a busy Overland Park thoroughfare before making a loop around a pond fronting the corporate headquarters of Garmin, the people that brought GPS systems to the dashboards of cars around the world. This was the same pond that I once considered as a final resting place before Dixie diverted my attention by terrorizing a careless Canadian goose.

I don't know what it is about this particular walk. Perhaps it's the pond where she occasionally immerses herself, the water fowl, or what they leave behind on the sidewalk (once considered dessert but no longer, thanks to a shrill "leave it" command). At the mere mention of a "Dixie Walk," she begins to pant at a rate that makes her sound less a dog and more like an obscene phone call.

Once out the door, her pace quickens and I am thrust into one of those funky power walk modes. To a passerby, it must appear as though my body is coming unhinged. Once we reach the pond, I disconnect the leash and she skips along the pond's edge in search of that which only she knows. On warm nights, her solitary front leg often cramps up as we make our way home causing an immediate cessation of all forward motion. Only Dixie decides when it is time to resume the walk.

Dixie Walks give me time to think. Much of this book was conceived on Dixie Walks. On this night, however, I had but one issue to resolve. Do I stay and appease my students? If so, I would risk another close encounter of the ugly kind with an overzealous detective. Then again, I could disappear into Iowan obscurity for the rest of my days. No one in my inner circle nor my employer had been contacted by investigators as to my whereabouts. The accusation was a fraud. Maybe that had become clear by now.

My students had cast the deciding vote. I would stay. The managers at the Cedar Rapids store were understandably disappointed. In retrospect, I believe it was a life-saving decision. After all, I wasn't going to Cedar Rapids to build a new life. I was going to Cedar Rapids to die at my own hands. It was just a question of when. And not even the site of Dixie going bowling for geese was going to change that.

"You gave me strength to stand alone again
To face the world out on my own again
You put me high upon a pedestal
So high that I could almost see eternity . . ."

Randy Goodrum, "You Needed Me"

CHAPTER 31: SYMBIOSIS

Regardless of where I landed, I could not escape the fallout from yet another setback. I walked on the opposite side of the street when people approached. At the dog park, I hugged the fence line to avoid contact with patrons. The site of a police car at the apartment complex sent me ducking for cover. I watched through closed blinds until the officer left while making sure I had an exit plan in the event she moved in my direction. Public appearances were rare and I spent most of the time at restaurants scanning the room for anyone giving me a second look. Why was I behaving this way? I hadn't done anything.

My dogs served as a conduit to the outside world. Dogs need at least thirty minutes of head hanging, tongue dragging exercise each day so the three of us jog at least three times a week. We hike the abundant nature trails throughout Kansas City and walk the neighborhood twice daily, sometimes more.

Dixie, Oreo, and I also frequent the many off-leash parks located throughout the Kansas City Metro. Oreo is a "chaser" and a bit of a loner. She's never met a scent that didn't intrigue her. I'm guessing she was a hound dog or a terrier in a former life. At best, she is a "wannabe" in this one. If I had a yard, Oreo would have already provided me with an 18-hole miniature golf course in her never ending quest for filet-o-rodent. She's the dog that will follow her nose for an hour and then look up to discover that she's wandered into another zip code. It is for that reason that she stays on leash everywhere but a dog park or fenced yard.

Dixie is a social butterfly when she is not 10 paces behind me. Children, adults, seniors or anyone with a cookie draws her attention though she never stays long enough to lose sight of me. She abhors ill-mannered dogs and gives a wide berth to the dust cloud that surrounds a canine scruff. Some days she plays the "lion and the wildebeest" game with Oreo. Dixie stalks while Oreo grazes and roots at the ground. At some point, Oreo will look up and go into a casual trot. Dixie springs from the savannah and the chase is on. The pursuit breaks off after about 20 yards when Oreo's speed elicits a disgruntled *"screw you"* from Dixie.

Before I leave for work, I stuff a Kong® or some treat dispensing puzzle toy for each dog and hide it in the apartment. When your home is less than 800 square feet, you can run out of hiding places pretty quickly. Some days, a Kong can be found in a shoe. I wear a size 13 so space is never a problem. Other times, a toy can be found just under the bed skirting or behind a door.

I've barely set foot in the parking lot before the search operation is underway. Once retrieved, the process of separating the treats from the Kong begins. To challenge them further, I place a sliver of peanut butter or vanilla yogurt in the Kong and then freeze it overnight. Once the Kong has been gutted, it's back to dozing which is no doubt followed by a nap. Without me, they are prisoners in my apartment and would surely die of loneliness, starvation or sheer boredom if I were not to return. They are forever dependent on me and that joyous responsibility leaves little time for pity parties.

A person's departure can trigger various levels of stress in a dog. For an increasing number, being alone can trigger a puppy panic attack known as separation anxiety. Dogs have been bred for thousands of years to be our companions. Is it any wonder that our exodus creates some measure of anxiety? Dixie and Oreo associate my departure with the aforementioned treasure hunt. But to say this ploy has rendered Dixie immune from of any stress related to my exits would be misleading.

Dixie was treated to day camp twice a week while I worked in the Overland Park PetSmart store. She was assigned to the front playroom which is visible to the sales floor. Dixie was reluctant to leave me at check-in, looking like a timid child on the first day of kindergarten. She was fine as long as she could not see me. But if my travels took me anywhere near the window facing the sales floor during my shift, she would bark and twirl incessantly until I disappeared from sight. If given the choice, Dixie would be at my side 24/7. She can live with being alone and Oreo has been a separation Band-Aid® for her along with the trusty Kong® toy. This, as well as her occasional bouts of reactivity, is the scratch in an otherwise shiny plate of armor.

Dogs need to be trained so I took them to the tennis courts at the apartment complex or a place called Loose Park for various on and off-leash exercises. Dixie has been certified twice as a Canine Good Citizen by the American Kennel Club, once in 2007 and again in 2011. In order to earn this certification, Dixie had to complete 10 obedience exercises flawlessly. I was confident in her ability to sit for a greeting, walk on a loose leash, heel through a crowd, "down" and "stay" but none too sure about greeting other dogs and something called "supervised separation."

In this exercise, I handed Dixie's leash to an evaluator and left the area for three minutes. During that time, Dixie could show no signs of stress or anxiety other than be mildly curious as to my whereabouts. She would have failed miserably had I been spotted but fortunately the drill required that I walk away. No problem.

Dixie even handled the dog greeting well, which has always been the case as long as the other dog is not out of control or, heaven forbid, trying to mount her. The late Jim Croce once penned these lyrics about a bar bully that eventually experienced some painful karma.

"You don't tug on Superman's cape
You don't spit into the wind
You don't pull the mask off the ol' Lone Ranger
And you don't mess around with Jim."

If I could rewrite that last line, it would read "and you don't mount a three legged dog."

A footnote: I am equally proud of Oreo for earning her "Canine Good Citizen" certification. This was quite an accomplishment for a frightened little dog who came to me untrained and under socialized. By no means is this a shameless self-promotion. This is about a little dog who faced down her fears and found the inner strength to be more than the sum of her life experiences. She now participates in rally obedience, a dog sport where handlers and their dogs walk through a course with 15-20 signs that instruct the team to perform various obedience exercises.

Oreo's personality is more cautious and reserved so I assumed agility would not be the sport for her. "Rally" moves slower and allows Oreo, for the most part, to move at her own pace. She loves to train and we practice almost daily. Good friends Jonathan and Jessica have built their own agility equipment for their adorable Pomeranians and set up a course in their yard. We visit Oliver and Cora almost weekly and each dog takes her turn through the course. Oreo has recently taken more interest in agility as I put Dixie through her paces. When it comes to dogs, you just never know.

Dogs need medical care so there were vet visits. I recall the first time Dixie was examined by our trusted vet, Dr. Barnes. After placing a stethoscope to her ribs, he turned to me and said "wow, she's got a big heart."

"You have no idea," I replied.

He does now.

Dogs need to be groomed. This was not a daunting task given that both Dixie and Oreo required little more than the occasional bath and nail trim along with a thorough brushing three times a week. Living in an apartment without access to a garden hose or a backyard left the tub as the only option for a doggie dip. It was cumbersome, not to mention messy. Thankfully, PetSmart has professional groomers and there were no better ones than the crew at the Overland Park store. Checking Dixie in usually resulted in a cat fight over whose turn it was to pamper my pooch.

I drew the line on excessive when I got a call one day asking if her nails could be painted. Use conditioner, spritz on some cologne if you must, but nail painting would not be permitted in our lifetime. I told this story to the Ward Parkway groomers who cared for Oreo and they promptly painted her nails red for Valentine's Day. I nearly had a stroke.

Dogs need attention from their companions and healthy interactions with strangers. I generally tried to avoid casual conversations with the human race away from the store unless the inquiry was about Dixie. This was inevitable whenever we wandered out. I pitied poor Oreo, as strangers would pander over Dixie while ignoring Oreo. As a final gesture of appeasement, I often heard "oh, and you're a nice dog too."

For a time, Oreo was patient and appeared unimpressed with the Dixie Admiration Society. One day at the dog park, however, Oreo went into a barking and growling fit as yet another group showered Dixie with affection. Oreo was uncharacteristically oblivious to my attempts at redirection and simply refused to be ignored. This tantrum plays out even today if Dixie becomes the subject of any conversation. I do little to correct her. It's Oreo's way of demanding equal time. Frankly, I think she's entitled. From Oreo's point of view, Dixie's fifteen minutes of fame are up. I must remind myself not to leave any copies of this book lying around. Oreo craves fiber in her diet.

I don't know how much money I've spent on Dixie and Oreo since October of 2005 when Dixie lurched her way into my heart. For my fiscal peace of mind, perhaps that's better left a mystery. According to the New York Times, some Americans spend upwards of $10,000 on pet services and supplies *per year*. Are there indulgences? Probably.

As stated earlier the pet industry has proven to be recession proof, generating 54 billion dollars a year in revenue. That's higher than the gross national product of all but nine African nations. In a recent survey where people were asked what they would be willing to sacrifice in an economic recession, everything from Starbucks to pedicures was mentioned. Internet service and the care of their pets were the two things people refused to concede.

Dixie and Oreo get Nutro Natural Choice kibble. It's certainly not a pricey holistic product but is a darn site better than the doggie "Twinkies®" found at grocery stores and super retailers. Bully sticks are great but they don't quite fit my budget lest I resign myself to a diet of "Spaghettios®" (been there, done that) so the girls "settle" for PetSmart generic rawhide chews. Dixie especially digs the rolls.

While neither of my dogs has ever seen the inside of a doggie resort, the girls visit the Stoll "off leash" park several times a week, have done dog day camp, and get a professional bath brush, and nail trim (minus the polish) every few months. These services provided me with a forum by which to playfully exploit Dixie's conditions.

For example, Dixie and I have become part of the initiation ritual for the new hires in both the grooming salon and the Pets Hotel. If Dixie has her nails trimmed by a newbie, I have been known to request a 25 percent discount while the veteran groomers giggle in the background.

One day a rookie receptionist asked if I was satisfied with the Pets Hotel services just as Dixie was being delivered to me.

"Well, she had four legs when I brought her in," I said in monotone.

"Hang on," replied the obviously flustered young woman. "I'll look in the back for you."

She left the company about two weeks later, no doubt for some intensive psychotherapy.

Dixie and Oreo accompany me everywhere dogs are allowed. Thankfully, Kansas City is a dog-friendly city on either side of the state line. As chronicled earlier, Dixie has hiked throughout the western US and even Canada. Oreo's first vacation was to Estes Park, Colorado in the summer of 2012. Did a mountain meadow produce some unbelievable poop to smell? I guess we all love the outdoors for different reasons.

Dixie and Oreo are the objects of my affection. Being single and living alone denies one the touch of another being. Scientists have studied the physiological effects of petting dogs in an attempt to qualify the therapeutic value of the human/dog bond. Mothers release a hormone known as oxytocin, for example, when nursing their infants. This is said to be the glue that bonds a mother to her child and is known as the "love hormone." Researchers have learned that oxytocin is produced in nearly equal quantities when people pet dogs. I must admit to feeling a wave of bliss myself as I gently stroke Dixie's velvet fur or rub Oreo's belly. The bottom line is that we all need to touch and be touched. Dixie and Oreo both enter doggie nirvana if you scratch in just the right place so the effect is not limited to our own species.

Having dogs in my life brings out the best qualities of a symbiotic relationship. My dogs quench my desire to nurture without the complications of bringing humans into the picture. In short, I need Dixie and Oreo in my life. It's a simple formula that works for us. One might argue after reading this book that Dixie is nothing more than a 1,200 mile umbilical cord to that little modular home in Arizona where Josh now resides. The reality is that a dog can never replace my son just as Josh could never be Dixie. Love is complicated, or perhaps uncomplicated, in that way. I'd like to think that there is room in my heart for both species. Love is in short enough supply. Why must it be monopolized by one species? Dixie and Oreo certainly don't see it that way.

Dixie and Oreo need me too. Most dogs are utterly dependent on us for their survival not only as pups but as adults. Domestication over the last 15,000 years has deprived many dogs of the skills necessary to be successful predators. Nowadays, dogs are scavengers as opposed to carnivores. I made several trips to Mexico to do volunteer work years ago and would observe packs of feral dogs not cooperatively hunting for fresh meat as their ancestors once did but rummaging around a landfill for scraps. Of course I hear tales of pet dogs that snag a bird in mid-flight or bring their owners the head of a baby squirrel but I think most of them got lucky. Though still equipped with teeth for tearing flesh, todays dogs primarily use them for gutting the stuffed pig we brought home from the Martha Stewart collection at PetSmart.

But how does Dixie feel about me? Am I the object of her affections or does she see me as a feeding trough? I proudly wear two shirts that speak to these points. One reads "Who adopted whom? Proud owner of a shelter dog." The other has these words stitched across the breast pocket "May I always be the kind of person my dog thinks I am."

Yes, Dixie chose me, as did Oreo. Your dog chose you. I believe this as if it were a universal truth. Though she was not at Helping Hands Humane Society very long, I wasn't the first person to pass by her kennel that October day back in 2005. From that point forward, the soul of the man and dog would be forever linked. Was that precise moment random or the result of some intelligent design? I lean towards the former but will not dismiss that latter. Start printing the bumper stickers: *"Love Happens"* (along with the other thing)."

> *"That's just the way it is*
> *Some things will never change*
> *That's just the way it is*
> *But don't you believe them . . ."*
>
> Bruce Honrsby, "That's Just the Way It Is"

CHAPTER 32: PET TRAINER CHRONICLES

As a pet trainer/educator, I have come to realize that the culture of dogs is as diverse as the various breeds recognized today by the American Kennel Club. While the majority of us view our dogs as beloved companions, many still subscribe to the legal definition that dogs are essentially property. Subscribing to this misguided perspective suggests that your dog is a lawn mower.

For example, a man came into the store and asked me if I trained dogs to attack. I replied that such a command did not exist in the PetSmart curriculum.

"What do you want him to attack?" I asked with tongue firmly planted in cheek.

"I have a pool," he deadpanned.

I was puzzled so decided to carry this pointless conversation to its inevitable conclusion.

"You're concerned that someone is going to steal your pool?"

"Oh no, I don't want no little kids coming around and falling in," he said with greater urgency in his voice.

The air brakes could no longer halt my raging sarcasm.

"You want your dog to maul the kid before he has a chance to drown in your pool? I get it now!"

The gentleman smiled and went about his business. I retreated to the rawhide aisle to gnaw on a femur bone.

On the other end of the relationship perspective is the anthropomorphic view. These folks invest a small fortune on grooming their Maltese to look more like their fraternal twin sister. I'm convinced that some dogs own more changes of clothes than I do. To accommodate (or enable) this philosophy, there are spas for dogs featuring pedicures, "Doga" (Yoga for dogs), and lodging that would impress a rock star. PetSmart Pet Hotel customers can purchase rooms with televisions that play your pet's favorite animal flicks. Do an Internet search for dog collars and you'll find more bling-bling than in a trendy shop on Fifth Avenue. For these people, having a dog is more about style than substance. Sadly, it's their "baby" that pays the ultimate price for these indulgences, for he yearns to be nothing more than a dog.

Of course there are those people that should never share their home with a dog in the first place.

A woman stopped me to ask where she could find the diapers. Yes, PetSmart and other retailers sell diapers for dogs. Some use them for potty training, others for males that mark or females during their heat cycle. They certainly make sense for older, incontinent dogs. I asked if she had any questions about the product.

"Not really," she said. "But I do have one question since you're a dog trainer. My little girl dog bleeds out her 'boo-boo' every month or so and I don't understand why she does that. My neighbor has a little girl dog about the same age and it never happens to her. Is she in winter or something?"

I paused in an attempt to operationally define "boo-boo" and "in winter."

"Ma'am, could it be that your dog is going through her menstrual cycle? Some have described this condition as being 'in season.' Could the reason your friend's dog no longer does this is because she has been spayed?"

Now it was the woman's turn translate.

"I have no idea" was the only reply she could muster and I walked away wondering if it was possible to sleep through an entire year of 7th grade biology.

Here's one for the ages. An 80 year old woman had enrolled in my training class. She relied on a walker for balance but was as lucid as a person half her age. Her daughter, overweight and appearing as though she needed a walker herself, had purchased an Australian shepherd puppy for her mother so that she would have a *companion*. I'm sure Aussies can assume this role as well as any dog if they have had logged 10 miles earlier in the day herding sheep.

"This dog is crazy, just crazy," the woman said on the first day of class. "I want you to train her to be an outside dog because she's too bad to be inside."

Other students in the class smiled awkwardly as I tried to make sense of what a trained outside dog would look like. Neither mother or daughter knew the breed of the dog so I took the liberty of pointing out just what Aussies were bred to do, then asked how often they were able to walk him. I figured we'd start with that.

"Well," she pondered, "we've only had her a month."

INSIGHTS: I AM NOT YOUR FUR BABY!

I've been a dog for longer than you know and it is my considered opinion that while many people love their dogs (to the degree that humans can), they are clueless as to how to care for us. Let's begin with a simple notion. Dogs are dogs. We are not people in fur coats. This notion of referring to our dogs as "fur babies" or "fur kids" fur-thers the myth that we are children with a tail and a wet nose. There is a fine line between pampering and spoiling so take notes while I try to explain each one.

The pampered pooch almost always gets what she needs in terms of food, shelter, and love. My best dog friends are pampered and we are happy dogs. Not everyone can afford bling-bling collars and leather leashes made from the hides of free roaming cattle. On the other hand, a spoiled dog controls more resources in the household than does her human roommates. Most of them wind up in Tim's training classes. Let me give you a glimpse into our world. We don't want to control your household. Heck, we have enough trouble figuring out where you want us to pee and why our name suddenly to changes to "damn dog."

What we *need* is someone to love and what we *want* is a human companion to care for us. As a friend who has discovered this wonderful new way to communicate with humans, let me give you some free advice.

Next time you visit the pet store, skip the aisles selling Harley Davidson vests and super hero t-shirts. Walk past the stinky stuff and the breath mints. We don't want to smell like you. We're dogs. We roll in poop. Sometimes we eat it. Try it sometime. You don't know what you're missing. By the way, we find human fragrances offensive which might explain why your dog looks like she's ready to hurl after catching a whiff of "Passion" by Elizabeth Taylor. One day there was a little Maltese that came into PetSmart. Her coat had been dyed hot pink. I'm not even going there.

I can't let this go without addressing the holidays and the ridiculous things you humans do to we loyal and faithful servants. The two greatest criminal acts occur at "Wear Strange Clothes and Scare the Crap Out of Us" day, "Get a Bunch of Junk You'll Never Use" day, and "Blow up Your Neighborhood" day.

Trust me, we don't belong at the community fireworks display dressed as Uncle Sam. I'll never understand why you spend so much money on enough TNT to bring down an airbus. When the noise makers lit up the desert sky, Tim would take me to the mountains where it was quiet and the crisp smell of the Ponderosa Pines was downright heavenly. It's flat where we live now and everyone wants to blow something up so we stay indoors. It's the one day out of the year I can count on a bone from the butcher shop.

For dogs, hordes of costumed little people on a sugar high and trusted adult companions who radically change their appearance spell anxiety with a capital "A." That sweet stuff you all come home with turns our intestines into a knot. Nowadays people insist on insidious costumes for their pets to wear. Each year, Tim begrudgingly hosts a costume contest at PetSmart. He smells like a bad mood when he comes home. Once I saw a basset hound dressed as a French Maid. Are you kidding me? Last year's winners were "Lips Lulu" and "Madame Margot," representatives of the oldest profession. Why do people force their dogs to wear things they wouldn't be caught dead in? Have you no shame?

Yes, I'm going to bag on the Merry/Happy holiday too. It's those photos with the hairy faced guy in a red suit. He seems to be everywhere, which is amazing considering he's plump and moves slowly, even for a human. Think about this from my point of view. Bring me to a strange place and sit me near a fat guy that only comes out of hibernation once a year. Now that I'm in the middle of a panic attack, force me to look directly into a single eye that stares me down like a wild predator just before I become the morning entrée. Scream my name, make silly noises to help me focus, and flash a blinding light in my eyes not once but several times. Pass the Prozac, please. By the way, can you help me strap on this Thunder Shirt?

Enough said.

We want to be with you a long time so give us regular check-ups with a vet. Buy us decent food that helps us feel full and poop less. Bring us inside with you so we can keep you company. We want to feel warm and safe too. Take us to school so we can learn what you want us to do. Making you happy is all we care about. Most of the time, we have no idea what you're saying to us. We're sniffing while you make strange sounds. Let's get on the same page. Finally, love us at least half as much as we love you. That's all any dog can ask from a human.

> *"Did you ever know that you're my hero?*
> *You're everything I wish I could be.*
> *I could fly higher than an eagle,*
> *For you are the wind beneath my wings . . ."*
>
> Jeff Silbar/Larry Henley, "Wind Beneath My Wings"

CHAPTER 33: HERO WORSHIP

Dustin and I went our separate ways upon my return from the Arizona debacle. Our lease had expired and he wanted to be closer to his fiancée. While sharing expenses had its financial advantages, I was thrilled about returning to a life with only canines for company. To his credit, Dustin could not have been a better roommate and I thoroughly enjoyed our time together. My life had become solitary and I was finally at peace with that.

I found an affordable two bedroom apartment just north of Overland Park in the tiny community of Mission. The second bedroom was for Josh in case he decided to come home. It was a shrine, of sorts. A shrine of hope that one day I would hear from him and we would be reunited as father and son. The apartment was an older brownstone with an open floor plan and my choice of colors for accent walls to personalize my new home. In a word, it was perfect. I asked about pet rent.

"We don't charge pet rent," said manager Amy. "Your dogs don't work, do they?"

"Where do I sign?" I replied, and the deal was done.

Although the nearest dog park was a twenty minute drive, there were plenty of suburban hikes available and a network of trails throughout the county that we had yet to explore. Kansas City is great that way. Both hiking and biking trails are abundant. They are clean, safe, and generally well maintained. The only things missing are mountains but Colorado is just a day's drive.

Lakes and woodlands are available for the catch and kill crowd. Those with a taste for the fine arts love the Nelson Art Gallery and Kauffman Center located near the famous Country Club Plaza. Party animals flock downtown to the Power and Light District or the Westport bar scene. Kansas City is also home to professional baseball, football, soccer, and hockey teams. College sports are but an hour to the east (University of Missouri) or west (University of Kansas). Both schools have satellite campuses in the city. There are community colleges, as well as private institutions and a number of vocational schools.

Kansas City is not a bad place to call home if you're a dog either. Three Dog Bakery and Brookside Barkery offer canine culinary delights. We have visited three dog parks in Missouri and three on the Kansas side of the state line. Dog day camp programs and classy boarding facilities are in abundance. Two periodicals are in circulation just for pet lovers. Dog events are scattered throughout the year and the Kansas City Pet Expo is a must-see event for people who think of their pet as more than just a yard ornament. All in all, Kansas City is well kept secret and I hope it stays that way.

While visiting the Greater Kansas City Pet Expo in April of 2011, I stumbled across an agility exhibition sponsored by the Dog Obedience Group, aka "DOG." I was familiar with the owners, Al and Jane, as they had hosted my internship with Animal Behavior College the year before. Lotta Sydanmaa, who taught the agility classes, invited Dixie and me to join them Friday evenings for an informal practice session.

I had checked with every agility instructor in the metro for the past year and could find no one who taught classes on Friday, Saturday, or Sunday nights. These were the only evenings I had available because of my schedule at PetSmart. I was working during the day both Saturday and Sunday so that wasn't an option. Our agility skills could use some fine tuning so I took Lotta up on her offer and made the 35 minute drive to Blue Springs, Missouri for the practice sessions.

Lotta is a native of Finland, although there is no trace of an accent in her voice. Tall and oozing with charisma, Lotta was the perfect spoil for our agility experience in Arizona. Dixie picked up where she left off, blowing through tunnels, bounding over jumps, and scaling the contacts as if they were speed bumps. The regulars marveled at her prowess and were stumped as to why NADAC wouldn't allow her to compete on each apparatus. Dixie had limited experience with the weave poles, but with Lotta's help, we slowly made progress on what many believe to be the toughest obstacle of them all. Then one Friday in November of 2011, Dixie experienced what could be best described as an agility epiphany. With just a flick of my wrist, she shimmied through the weave poles as though she had been doing it all her life. Her face was positively radiant that night.

"I get it now—I get it!" she seemed to be saying.

Somehow, it all started to make sense to her and she's never looked back.

It had been almost two years since Dixie and I competed. We registered for a trial at the same facility in Lawrence, KS that produced Dixie's first and only ribbon. The "hoops" competition was on Friday evening. I so much wanted to run tunnels again but that event was scheduled for Sunday and, of course, I had to work. I had watched the dogs run hoops as a spectator but could never really wrap my head around it. Lotta had entered her dog Marley and we walked the course together while choreographing each maneuver; a front cross here, a rear cross there, followed by a blind cross. What the hell? We had nothing to lose by trying.

Dixie flew through more hoops than I could count but missed one. It was my fault, as I had failed to commit her to the hoop before moving onto the next one. Staying ahead of a three legged dog is not a walk in the park. That's my excuse and I'm sticking with it.

We checked the results. Second place! With little practice time, virtually no formal training since 2009, and in an event she had never entered, Dixie managed to pull off a second place finish. She would probably have won the damn thing if it were not for handler error. Dixie was the Rocky Balboa of dogdom. She had made a remarkable comeback and I was more eager than ever to compete in the next trial scheduled for St. Patrick's Day weekend 2012. Eagerness was not something I had felt since that dreadful e-mail from Yvonne.

The local club that sponsors the agility competitions is called "U2 Kan Du Agility" and is run by pair of kindred spirits, Martha and Matt McCarter. Each event features a "fun run" where teams pay for five minutes on the course alone prior to the start of the trial. I quickly learned that the fee is waived for volunteers who arrive early to help Martha and Matt stage the event so this has been our practice. As with most dog sports, agility is not cheap and pinching pennies is a must on a retail budget like mine.

March followed an unusually mild Kansas winter in 2012 and Dixie was ready. I threw caution to the wind and entered her in hoops and took a Sunday off so she could run through her beloved tunnels. I even entered the weavers competition. I couldn't wait to get that one over with. Thankfully, it was Friday night. Dixie was a Cracker Jack agility competitor. As a handler, I was very much a work in progress. Thankfully, Dixie has been infinitely patient with me. Regardless of the results, we would be better for the experience.

After some time on the "fun run" course, Dixie was primed for the hoops. Midway through her run, Dixie suffered from an acute bout of puppy exuberance and jumped on me, nearly resulting in a disqualification. The judge was merciful, however, and she completed a near flawless run. Just as before, we eagerly waited until the results were posted. Not only did this now eight year old dog win first place, but she earned a qualifying run. Just two more "q's" and she would earn a title and be eligible to move into the "open" division. I was overjoyed but it was short lived, for up next was the dreaded weavers course.

It was no picnic. The course layout was difficult. Not only were there multiple sets of weave poles but hoops and tunnels to navigate as well. Between my obvious lack of technique and Dixie's rush to complete the course, she skipped poles and had to start back at the entry point. It seemed to take an eternity reach the final obstacle and I wondered if we would wind up on someone's blooper reel.

"Nice try Dix, but that really sucked," I joked as we left the course.

The other handlers were having the same difficulty with their dogs and suddenly our first stab at weavers didn't seem so brutal. I was mildly curious to check the results and was slack-jawed at what I found—second place. It had to be a typo. Nope, a red ribbon to add to the blue as well as the larger purple ribbon given to only those with qualifying runs. Tunnelers were next but not until Sunday and I was confident Dixie would set the world on fire. As usual, she did not disappoint.

I entered Dixie in two rounds of tunnelers. The first one was as clean as any she has ever completed, even at practice. The final leg of the course featured three tunnels in a line that turned the last 20 yards into a dead sprint and Dixie crossed the finish line like Secretariat, earning a blue ribbon as well as a qualifying run. Although the second run was not as clean, Dixie still managed to "q" while earning another first place. Our purse for the weekend: Three first place finishes; three qualifying runs; and a second place finish (mostly by default). I had to chuckle under my breath as a competitor looked at her dog after less than a stellar run and scolded "I can't believe you got beat by a three legged dog!"

"I will remember you
Will you remember me?
Don't let your life pass you by
Weep not for the memories . . .

Sarah McLachlan, *"I Will Remember You"*

CHAPTER 34: THE SOUL OF A DOG

Amber and her Weimaraner Fiona were students in a PetSmart "Beginner" obedience class that I taught in the spring of 2012. We first met out on the sales floor. Poor Fiona had been used as a breeder dog in a "puppy mill." Most of her life had been spent in a kennel producing multiple litters of puppies that were in turn sold to pet stores all over the country. She would not look at me, cowered as I approached, and refused to take even the most delectable treat from my hand.

Experts estimate that there are 3,000 puppy mills in the "Show Me" state alone. They supply 80 percent of the puppies sold in retail stores. Law enforcement along with animal welfare advocates such as the American Society for the Prevention of Cruelty to Animals (ASPCA) and the Human Society of the United States have joined forces to enact legislation to more closely regulate the treatment of the animals in these facilities.

Puppy mills produce genetically flawed and often unhealthy puppies that the impulsive public purchases at ridiculous mark ups and brings into their homes. Those like Fiona who spend a lifetime reproducing are emotionally traumatized and physically fragile dogs. They are under-socialized and often sickly. If they are fortunate enough to be delivered from this breeding underworld, they are essentially damaged goods.

Amber was a social work student and planned to spend her life rehabilitating broken people. Adopting Fiona seemed like a perfect fit. It was a slow go in the beginning. Fiona was terrified inside a busy pet retailer and overwhelmed with a classroom full of strangers. While teams practiced sits, downs, and stays, Fiona hunkered down in a corner of the room looking away from all that moved in her direction. But Amber was patient and Amber was kind and Amber was persistent. Soon, Fiona began to respond. My students celebrated her every accomplishment. By week five of a six week class, Fiona could perform the same behaviors as her classmates that had never lived her life.

The final week of a Beginner class is largely a review session with a few games and tricks thrown in for fun. Amber and Fiona never missed class but they were noticeably absent on this Wednesday night. On Saturday, Amber's roommate came into the store to deliver the news. Fiona died. She had been hit by a car.

Amber thought Fiona had wandered off to visit a neighbor. In fact, she had crossed the street to visit someone else. When Amber called Fiona, Amber thought that she was but a few feet away. Fiona responded to her name and crossed the busy street. She was struck and then dragged for several feet as Amber screamed in horror. The veterinarian at the emergency clinic determined that Fiona's internal injuries left little hope for a full recovery and Amber gave her dog the ultimate gift and ended her suffering.

As a social work professional, Amber had offered grief counseling to others. Now she found herself in need of her own services. Fiona was not just a rehabilitation project. She took residence in the corner apartment of Amber's heart where a "for rent" sign now hung.

Such is the depth of the relationship many of us have with our dogs. It is to be rejoiced and celebrated. The only downside to sharing my life with dogs is that they don't live long enough. Fiona taught Amber to savor each moment for we know their lives to be more finite than even our own. Would we come home from work just a little bit earlier in the day if we knew our children would be senior citizens by the time they turned 10?

I guess dog lovers are masochists of a sort. We can't remember there not being a dog in our home so we grieve at their passing only to eventually acquire another. And another. And each time they leave our world, we stitch together the tattered pieces of our heart only to do it all over again.

Hans, or "Hanzie" as I called him, was my first dog. There are pictures of me as an infant curled up in Hanzie's basket while he watched over me from inside my playpen. Mom had a penchant for boxers but they were too rambunctious for a family with a baby so she settled on a standard dachshund. Hanzie cheerfully tolerated my ear tugs and tail yanks until I was old enough to know better. He developed back problems later in life. To this moment, I can recall the day I came home from school and Mom sat me down with younger sister Amy and fought through her own grief as she explained that Hanzie had died earlier in the day.

Tears welled up in my eyes and I bounded out the front door to find the afternoon football scruff. The guys must have thought I was possessed as I launched myself like a missile into the ball carrier or anyone trying to bring me down when it was my turn to play offense. The thought of Hanzie never coming home left me angry and confused. The physicality of football had temporarily exorcised the pain but I cried at night for months. As is the case with many children, the loss of a beloved pet was my first encounter with death.

Next came Hildegard, or Hilde. Mom always thought that a dog with German roots should carry a strong German name. My younger sister Amy was away at Girl Scout camp for the weekend and I remember Mom saying "we're only going to look, not buy." In my mind, that ranks right up there with "it will only hurt a little" and "some assembly required."

Hilde was comical, submissive, and rather portly as dachshunds go. I adored her as she did me. She loved people and the depth of that love could be measured in the amount or urine she would release upon greeting people. The neighbor lady, Mrs. Parmenter, could empty Hilde's bladder by simply speaking her name from fifty yards away. Hilde passed away while I was away at college. I was so distraught that I skipped classes that day and I *never* cut class. Nothing really seemed to matter for days after that. I loved the independence that was my college life but would have traded a year of it to be with Hilde when she died.

After Hilde came Missy, on "Mini-mutt," as Dad used to call her. As it turned out, the German name thing didn't last beyond the first two wiener dogs. I guess Helga just didn't strike a chord with Mom. I was perhaps less familiar with her, as I was living in Arizona during her best years. Sadly, her life was shortened by cancer, but she was Mom's constant companion through some lonely years following her divorce from my father. Missy had a reptilian tongue that could penetrate any orifice of the body. I used to lay face down on the floor, cover my ears and sing "miniminiminimini" as that crazy tongue probed for any opening she could find. When Missy died, Mom swore it was the last dog she would ever own. She could not bear to go through the loss of another beloved "dachsie."

At my urging, we responded to an ad in the local paper for dachshund puppies some months later.

"We're only going to look. You're under no obligation to buy," I said one day with tongue firmly planted in cheek. She smiled and Maggie was home and sitting on her lap three hours later.

Maggie has been Mom's roommate for 12 years. Her favorite toy is a squeaky soccer ball which she retrieves from a wicker trash can by tipping it over and waiting for the ball to roll out. It's her only trick and Mom amuses guests with it at every opportunity. Mom is 82 and I believe Maggie will be her last dog. Our family has been enriched by every dachshund that has shared our home.

The aforementioned Princess was *my* first dog. I was 26 and dating the woman that would one day be my wife and Josh's mother. Yvonne's mother Nancy had a friend who was trying to unload a litter of yellow lab puppies and the last one found its way into Nancy's home just before Christmas 1986. Nancy, however, loved Cocker Spaniels and we had already acquired a chocolate Cocker as a Christmas gift when Princess unexpectedly arrived on the scene. Yvonne and I were without a dog so we became the caretaker of a little yellow puppy. Princess was an absolute gem of a dog; playful, obedient, and outgoing. She shared my love of the outdoors. Together we hiked north central Arizona, played fetch in the park, jogged, and hung out while Yvonne worked various night jobs.

It was the smile that was her most endearing feature. Yes, a smile. We trainers refer to it as a submissive grin. Princess greeted me daily with a bob of the head, followed by a curl of her upper lip and a snort that released a shower of slobber if you were in range. Get close enough and you're going to get wet. It's sort of like sitting in the area marked "splash zone" at Sea World. If she thought she was in trouble, Princess would curl the lip and hiss like a coiled rattle snake. These "grins" kept unknowing strangers on edge, Bible thumpers at bay, and sent more than one UPS driver scurrying for his brown van.

Knowing what I do today, I must confess to having been a dog guardian of moronic proportions. Princess ate crap. Translation; whatever was on sale at the grocery store. She rode unrestrained in the back of my Toyota pickup, often on the highway. I was not vigilant about applying flea and tick preventive treatments or heart worm pills. She spent way too much time outside, even on inclement days. Yet through my unforgiveable ignorance, Princess' devotion was a constant in my life for 13 years. I'm sorry, old girl. I should have done better by you. Please know that you were a cherished companion and a treasured friend. Your selfless love led me to Dixie.

W. Bruce Cameron is an enormously gifted author whose books, "A Dog's Purpose" and "A Dog's Journey" have had a profound impact on my understanding of the canine spirit. In these beautifully sculpted stories, Cameron chronicles the life of one dog's soul through multiple lifetimes as he searches for his purpose. It is the author's premise that a dog carries her previous memories and experiences into the next life until her work on Earth is complete.

Could it be that Cameron is onto something here? How I wish it could be true. Do our dogs weave a thread of love through the tapestry of our lives? Hans was the dog off my childhood; Hilde, the dog of my adolescence; Princess, the dog of my young adult years; and Dixie, the dog of my life. I would like to believe that they are but one soul; existing in multiple bodies throughout our lifetime, whose only purpose is to keep us warm, safe and loved. Is this random or a product of intelligent design? This time I will go with the latter. After all, dog is God spelled backwards.

To extend the metaphor, perhaps Oreo's journey began with me. When she dies, will she be reborn to care for someone dear to me? Josh, perhaps? That single thread now becomes a capillary, extending a lineage of love in all directions to bring light to an increasingly barren world.

"Your life is now
In this undiscovered moment
Lift your head up above the crowd . . ."

John Mellencamp, *"Your Life Is Now"*

CHAPTER 35: FOREVER IN A MOMENT

I once said this memoir would be unlike most others in that the dog wouldn't die in the end. Events in 2012, however, nearly made a liar out of me. Years ago, Dixie had a benign tumor removed from the top of her head near her right ear. The incision was sewn and subsequently popped open on the way home from the clinic where Dixie received veterinary care at that time. Sutures were replaced with staples and I playfully nicknamed her "Franken-dog." Unfortunately, the hair never grew back, leaving her with an unsightly bald spot not unlike the one at the top of my cranium.

No more than a couple of years passed before another lump appeared on her right shoulder. Dr. Barnes suspected it was benign as well but encouraged me to watch it carefully. If it began to grow, it was worth another look. In the spring of 2012, Dixie came to the store to do some demonstrations with a newly hired pet trainer. Stopping to visit store manager Kathy was always the first order of business for Dixie. As Kathy stroked her baby soft coat, her hand suddenly stopped. Kathy knew Dixie's medical history as if she were her own child.

"It's getting bigger," she said in a somber tone. "I can tell."

I reached down to feel the lump. In fact, it *had* grown. I called Dr. Barnes immediately and made an appointment for the following week. Dixie was a model patient and today was no different. She sat quietly while Dr. Barnes measured the lump. It was approximately a half inch larger than the previous measurement recorded in Dixie's file. The lump would need to be extracted and Dixie was scheduled for surgery. Once removed, the mass would be sent to a lab (no, not that kind of lab!) for further analysis.

The call came on the first Friday in April 2012. The lump on her back turned out to be a level one mast cell tumor. It was cancer. The Big C. Thankfully, the prognosis for a level one tumor is very optimistic. Once the mass is removed, the animal is usually cancer free and such was the case with Dixie. For now, Death had taken a holiday.

Shawnee Mission Park is a mecca for any outdoor enthusiast. It spans more than 1,200 acres in Johnson County, Kansas and is easily accessible from anywhere in the Metro. Whether your hobby is flying model aircraft or disc golf, you can do it at Shawnee Mission Park. The lake is home to the anglers and boaters. There's a beach and even an area for swimming set aside for dogs. Bike trails extend through the park and northward to the Kansas River. Brian and I have ridden them many times. Dixie and I, and most recently Oreo, enjoy the hiking trails that provided a scenic respite from city life. Oreo, forever the hound dog "wannabe," remains on a leash while Dixie forges ahead like a runaway snow plow. The scar from her surgery was a month old and the sutures had been removed. Much to her dismay, I had limited Dixie's activity during her convalescence so she was itching to get out of my apartment.

It was a Sunday evening after work and Brian joined us for this three mile trek through the woods. We had just passed the halfway point when it occurred to me that I hadn't seen Dixie for a while. I called out, which usually produced a rumbling in the brush but this time there was only eerie silence. Poison ivy lined the trail on either side so bushwhacking wasn't an option at this point. We backtracked a bit and I called out again. No Dixie. Now I was getting worried and Brian could tell. Though he had lived with dogs, he was not the doggie devotee that I had become. Like a true friend, he understood the depth of my feelings for my furry companions even if he didn't share them.

We decided to complete the hike. The trail ended where it began and I knew that Dixie's built-in GPS would eventually lead her back to the truck. Brian kept the conversation light and tried desperately to humor me as my pace quickened.

There was no sign of Dixie when we arrived back at the trailhead. I could feel the tightness in my chest as I pondered our next move. Maybe she was injured and was lying motionless in the brush along the trail. Maybe she had been attacked by a stray coyote or kicked by a deer. Though unlikely, maybe she was even lost. She had never wandered off like this. Suddenly my cell rang and a young lady said she had my dog about a half mile up the road. Dixie had made her way back to the trail head.

Unfortunately, it was a trail we had hiked the week before. She was sitting quite contently with three teens as Brian and I pulled up then charged me like a raging bull when she heard my voice. I didn't know whether to embrace her or box her ears. When Josh was around 4, he strayed at Wal-Mart and a security guard found him in the women's lingerie section. It's that "I'm so glad you're safe, now what the hell were you thinking?" feeling.

These incidents served to remind me that Dixie's time on this earth and with me is finite. It is linear. There is a beginning, middle, and an end and I have no control over the latter. I could lose Dixie to cancer. She could wander away on some trail and never return. Maybe she will have another close encounter with a car. Who knows, she could even outlive me for I know not what tomorrow brings.

If misery loves company, so, apparently, does adversity and redemption.

The ancient Greek philosophers described love in three ways (and sometimes a fourth). *Eros* is erotic love such as the passion we might feel for a life partner. *Philia* is said to be the love one feels for a family member or friend. It is what those fortunate enough to be in relationship with a dog experience daily. *Agape* is unconditional love that requires the ultimate sacrifice to be made in its name. This, I believe, is what our dogs feel for us. Look at the world around you and tell me who is more evolved?

It is true that I am not the same person today that I was before those dreadful events of 2006 and 2010. Once the extrovert, I am guarded and distant with strangers. There was a day when I fancied myself an amateur thespian. Nowadays I do little to draw attention to myself and abhor crowds.

I write letters to Josh but not as many as I used to. Of course they go unanswered. There was a time when I called weekly but grew weary of my ex-wife's voice instructing me to leave a message with the assurance that the call would be returned. Rarely was that the case so I no longer play that game.

It's been more than two years since I have lain eyes on my son. I know nothing about his life, his loves, or what inspires him. I may never see him again. I may never meet the woman he loves. I may never hold my grandchildren. His face will likely not be the last thing I see when I leave this world. I wish I had been a better father.

My inner circle has remained constant through the turmoil of the past several years. Though I prefer the company of my dogs to most people, my friends help me keep one foot firmly planted in humanity. Thankfully, their loyalty was never tested again. No investigation surfaced from the Arizona accusation.

Dixie earned a title in the "hoopers" competition in June of 2012. In August, she took home a title in tunnelers while adding another "q" in weavers. Our goal is to earn a title in every event for which she is allowed to compete. This would be the crowning achievement of her agility career. Even if she never runs again, man and dog are so much the better for the shared experience. Victory gives us cause to celebrate a moment. The journey continues.

You can't even dream this stuff. The very idea that my girl entered an athletic competition against normal dogs half her age and won boggles the mind. They have a word for that.

Extraordinary.

Dixie and I have both lost something that can never be replaced and for that we are irrevocably changed. In Dixie's case, it was an appendage. A new leg will not emerge from the scar near her chest. My loss was an appendage of sorts too, for my son and my former career were essentially extensions of my soul. Together, Dixie and I have learned to live with what we have tragically lost. The lesson here is that we are only shaped by those events, not defined by them. It has been a journey of discovery and mutual healing.

By walking the path together, we have redefined our lives. Dixie is my companion. She is an emerging agility champion and she is the official PetSmart morale officer. I am the guardian of two wonderful dogs. I have the privilege of being my mother's son and a friend to some truly remarkable people. I am a pet trainer/educator and an amateur writer. I'd like to think I'm still a dad. Through hardship we have discovered redemption. With redemption, there is hope. Where there is hope, one can again find the joy in living each moment of each day.

I stay home more and have therefore have learned to be comfortable in my own skin. I prefer the company of my dogs to most people I know. Though never one to indulge in luxuries, I have downsized my life. Today I celebrate in the simple pleasures of lunch with a friend; the trees in autumn; the wind in my face on a downhill bike ride; a mountain hike in spring time; and the expression of utter joy on the faces of my dogs when I come home from work. Despite what has been taken from us, we are whole again as long as we have each other. These are lessons I have learned over the past eight years from a 53 pound yellow Lab once considered a "disposable dog." Oreo's gift of love and devotion has been an affirmation to what Dixie has taught me and has helped to make me a better human being.

Some might argue that I am emotionally dependent on a dog. The very notion implies weakness, dysfunction, perhaps even mental illness. Perhaps, though, the times are changing. Doctors now prescribe dogs as remedies for legitimate emotional maladies such as depression and post-traumatic stress disorder. Unfortunately, the Department of Justice says they must be able to pick up a set of keys and turn on a light switch to be classified as a service dog. Therapeutic value isn't enough. Once again, dogs are property in the eyes of the law. All I know is that no pill could have saved me from myself in 2006. I needed stronger medicine. I needed Dixie.

I am not alone. Captain Luis Carlos Montalvan suffered physical wounds, traumatic brain injury, and the crippling effects of post-traumatic stress after two tours of duty in Iraq. His memoir, "Until Tuesday," tells the story of a battle on his home front. Because his injuries were not always visible, society would not accept his Golden Retriever Tuesday as a service dog. Time and again, this decorated Army veteran was verbally harassed, banned from public places and dismissed as being less than a man for having a dog at his side. Blades wielded by the intolerant sometimes cut the deepest.

Maybe I was emotionally dependent on Dixie. There is no shame in admitting that. Today, I prefer to think that I am emotionally *connected* to Dixie and Oreo. My capacity for love is not limited to the humanoid life forms. Only human arrogance serves as judge and jury in matters of love.

Dixie begins her night in my bed along with Oreo. She bides her time until I nod off and then sails into to multiple ports through the evening such as my oversized recliner, the couch, the area rug on the living room floor, and her bed. Inevitably I greet the morning with Dixie's muzzle pressed against my arm. Oreo maintains a constant vigil at my side during the night. If I were five years old, she would be the stuffed Panda bear of my childhood named Sam. Come to think of it, Oreo sort of looks like Sam. Black on white, or is it white on black?

I have always been a morning person and often get more done by noon than some do in a day. But on this morning I am vacationing just outside Rocky Mountain National Park. Yesterday, I hiked along the Continental Divide then took an afternoon stroll with Dixie and Oreo in the National Forest just outside Estes Park, Colorado. My legs feel like stone and I am not so quick to jump out of the sack. It is daybreak at 7,000 feet and I quietly entertain the notion that I died during the night and I am waking up in an idyllic afterlife. I open my eyes to a morning as still as the mountain lake we discovered the day before. Oreo is curled in a fetal position at my left hip. Beside me is Dixie, where she has always been. She will forever be with me in spirit, mind, and body. She exists for me in a way that no one else can.

Hers is the face of contentment and together we watch the sunrise over the peaks from the comfort of a queen sized bed. Serenity is ours for the taking as the world becomes mute. Dixie has taught me to breathe in and revel in this moment.

For it will never come again.

DIXIE'S APPENDIX

(No, not THAT appendix)

I hate cell phones. So do my friends. More specifically, I hate what humans have become as a result of them. Maybe that explains why your 5-G was recently chewed up like an old slipper. You have food at home yet you leave us alone so you can eat with strangers. That part never made sense to me. What I find more bewildering is when mom, dad, and the kids go to these places and poke their fingers into these silly little boxes. They all sit at the same table and never once do they talk to one another.

People never look where they are going these days. I remember a woman once stepped on Oreo. She was staring into her hand and never saw Oreo sitting at the curb. Oreo shrieked and she spilled her drink. Tim covered his mouth and suddenly the soda he was drinking started coming out his nose. Never saw that before. I just panted and smiled. In case you didn't know, that's how dogs laugh.

I always thought humans would by happy in a pet store. First, there are the succulent smells of food in all directions. Secondly, there are dogs attached to their people. Sometimes I think people would get lost if they weren't connected to a dog. Third . . . well, I can't get past the first two so I'll stop with food and dogs.

On this day the people at the pet store were not so happy. Just before Tim and I were to go home, a distraught woman ran towards the hospital holding a badly injured Yorkie in her arms. There was a crowd standing around a police officer explaining that a car had hit the little guy. I don't understand why a car would want to hit a dog. Believe me when I tell you that cars are the skin of evil. Maybe that's why some of my friends try to chase them away.

I heard one man say that the Yorkie was not wearing his leash while the lady was talking on her phone. After the doctor took the dog back to the "this will only hurt for a second" room, the woman demanded the officer arrest the man that drove the car. The man seemed afraid of the woman and apologized to her and to the police officer. I thought that was very kind of him since it was actually the car that committed the crime. The officer turned to the man and said he was free to go. He gave the woman a piece of pretty yellow paper. Humans love green pieces of paper so I thought the woman would be thrilled. Instead, she snapped the paper from the officer's hand and mumbled some ugly words. I could smell the anger on her breath from across the store.

The doctor fixed her little dog and I thought this would make her happy but she remained angry, especially after the lady at the front desk gave her more papers. These papers were white and I am assuming she did not like them because they weren't green like the ones she was taking out of her purse.

I met an old dog at the park once and he told me of a time when people did not have boxes in their hand and they spent a lot less time on the phone. Every home I've ever visited comes with a screen of slow moving images. People sit in their chairs and stare at these screens for hours on end. Our screen hardly ever glows which means that Tim has more time for me.

Half the dogs I see these days are too big for their skin. I think this is because they have nothing else to do but sleep while their humans talk on their phones, go palm poking, and watch the images on the big screen. Humans and dogs have been best friends since forever. We take care of you and you take care of us. Nowadays, gadgets seem to be taking care of people. What's a dog to do but lie around, pass gas, and get fat?

We want our job back. The bond between us is weakening. Unplug from your gadgets and you will reconnect with us, not to mention the people you love.

###